The
END TIMES
IN
CHRONOLOGICAL
ORDER

RON RHODES

HARVEST HOUSE PUBLISHERS
EUGENE, OREGON

THE END TIMES IN CHRONOLOGICAL ORDER
Copyright © 2012 by Ron Rhodes
Published by Harvest House Publishers
Eugene, Oregon 97402
www.harvesthousepublishers.com

Library of Congress Cataloging-in-Publication Data
Rhodes, Ron.
   The end times in chronological order / Ron Rhodes.
      p. cm.
   Includes bibliographical references (p.   ).
   ISBN 978-0-7369-3778-8 (pbk.)
   ISBN 978-0-7369-4263-8 (eBook)
   1. Bible—Prophecies—End of the world. 2. End of the world—Biblical teaching. 3. Bible—Prophecies—Chronology. I. Title.
   BS649.E63R52 2012
   236'.9—dc23

                                                                          2011042310

To my son, David

Acknowledgments

I wish to publicly acknowledge and thank the late Dr. John F. Walvoord, my primary prophecy mentor at Dallas Theological Seminary (DTS) in the 1980s. I also continue to appreciate Dr. J. Dwight Pentecost at DTS for his comprehensive courses on the prophetic books of Daniel and Revelation. The insightful teachings of Walvoord and Pentecost played a significant role in shaping my views on biblical prophecy.

I am also brimming with gratitude for my wife, Kerri, not only for the blessing she is in my life today but also for the blessing she was during my seven years of graduate study at DTS. From the very beginning, she has faithfully stood by me and my work, and I could not have engaged in this life of ministry without her.

Finally, I remain eternally grateful to the Lord for blessing Kerri and me with two wonderful children—David and Kylie, both now grown—whose lives and Christian commitment are never-ending sources of inspiration. Even as I write, David is busy taking seminary courses, and Kylie just returned from missionary work in Ghana.

Praise to the Lord for His many blessings!

Contents

Preface

Thank you for reading this book. I hope it proves to be a blessing to you!

To get the most out of it, you need to understand its layout. Each chapter deals with the events in a particular time period in God's prophetic plan, and the chapters are in chronological order. The specific prophetic events within each chapter are also arranged chronologically. The opening page of each chapter lists the events in the chapter, so navigating through the book is easy. The book is designed to be a user-friendly chronological guide to end-times biblical prophecy.

In some cases, the actual chronology of a prophetic event is based more on theological inferences than on explicit biblical statements. In view of this, there is room for some disagreement among Christians regarding the timing of some prophetic events. The chronology expressed in this book is faithful to the biblical text, based on a literal interpretation of prophecy, and held by many devout believers in God's Word.

My prayer is that this book will help you to understand God's plan for the ages. I hope it will also help you get excited about God's Word!

Ron Rhodes
Frisco, TX
2011

1

Introduction to
Biblical Prophecy

You Can Trust Prophetic Scripture

We are living in strange times. One very popular and influential author—an Emergent Christian—says we cannot be certain about anything, including such biblical doctrines as prophecy. We should therefore dismiss any concern for such things as evidence, proof, debate, and arguing for one position over another. All is ambiguous, we are told.

As I read this author's book, it struck me that one paragraph after another was brimming with self-defeating arguments. For example, he seemed completely certain that he was correct about his position that we cannot be certain about anything.

He also asserted that there are no good reasons for what we believe—and then provided what he considered to be good reasons for holding that there are no good reasons for what we believe. This kind of sloppy thinking is a reflection of our current culture.

A Certain and Trustworthy Revelation

In the Scriptures, God has provided everything He wants us to know about Him and how we can have a relationship with Him. God is the one who caused the Bible to be written. Through it He speaks to us today just as He spoke to people in ancient times when its words were first given.

We are to receive the Bible as God's words to us and revere and obey them as such. As we submit to the Bible's authority, we place ourselves under the authority of the living God.

The Bible is not merely a human product—it is God-inspired. Inspiration does not mean simply that the biblical writer felt enthusiastic, like the composer of the "Star Spangled Banner." The biblical Greek word for inspiration literally means "God-breathed." Because Scripture is breathed out by God—because it originates from Him—it is true.

Biblical inspiration may be defined as God's superintending of the human authors so that, using their own individual personalities and even their writing styles, they composed and recorded without error His revelation to humankind in the words of the original manuscripts. In other words, the original documents of the Bible were written by men who were permitted to exercise their own personalities and literary talents but who wrote under the control and guidance of the Holy Spirit, the result being a perfect and errorless recording of the exact message God desired to give to humankind.

Both the Old and New Testaments repeatedly claim to be of divine origin. In Zechariah 7:12, for example, the prophet refers to "the law and the words that the Lord of hosts had sent by his Spirit through the former prophets." This is a claim that the writings ("words") of Moses and the Old Testament prophets were of divine origin.

Likewise, in 2 Samuel 23:2, David wrote, "The Spirit of the Lord speaks by me; his word is on my tongue." Both the divine origin and the human instrument of Scripture are mentioned here. The writings came from God but were mediated through a prophet of God.

The apostle Paul in 2 Timothy 3:16-17 likewise affirms that Scripture comes from God: "All Scripture is breathed out by God and profitable for teaching, for reproof, for correction, and for training in righteousness, that the man of God may be competent, equipped for every good work." Several things are important in this text. First, Paul refers to "all Scripture" (the entire Old Testament), which Timothy learned from his Jewish parentage (verse 15). Second, the actual written text has divine authority—the "Scripture" (Greek: *grapha*). Third, these writings were inspired, or more literally, "God-breathed." Finally, they have divine authority for faith and practice. Because they are the Word of God, they are authoritative for the people of God.

Second Peter 1:21 provides a key insight regarding the human—divine interchange in the process of inspiration. This verse informs us that "no prophecy was ever produced by the will of man, but men spoke from God as they were carried along by the Holy Spirit." The Greek word translated "carried along" literally means "forcefully borne along." Even though human beings were used in the process of writing down God's prophecies, these men were all literally borne along by the Holy Spirit. The human wills of the authors were not the originators of God's message. God did not permit the will of sinful human beings to misdirect or erroneously record His message. Put another way, God *moved*, and the prophet *mouthed* these revealed truths. God *revealed* and man *recorded* His Word to humankind.[1]

Interestingly, the Greek word translated "carried along" in 2 Peter 1:21 is also found in Acts 27:15-17. In this passage the experienced sailors could not navigate the ship because the wind was so strong. The ship was being driven, directed, and carried along by the wind. This is similar to the Spirit's driving, directing, and carrying the human authors of the Bible as He wished. The word is a strong one, indicating the Spirit's complete superintendence of the human authors.

Yet just as the sailors were active on the ship (though the wind, not the sailors, ultimately controlled the ship's movement), so the human authors were active in writing as the Spirit directed. This assures us that the prophetic Scriptures truly did derive from God and not mere human beings.

Jesus Confirms the Divine Authority of Scripture

Christ Himself indicated we can fully trust the prophetic Scriptures. His view of Scripture can be stated briefly in six statements:

1. Scripture is divinely authoritative. Jesus Himself declared to Satan, "It is written, 'Man shall not live by bread alone, but by every word that comes from the mouth of God'" (Matthew 4:4).

2. Scripture is imperishable. Jesus declared, "Do not think that I have come to abolish the Law or the Prophets; I have not come to abolish them but to fulfill them. For truly, I say to you, until heaven and earth pass away, not an iota, not a dot, will pass from the Law until all is accomplished" (Matthew 5:17-18).

3. Scripture is infallible. Jesus clearly affirmed that "Scripture cannot be broken" (John 10:35).

4. Scripture is inerrant. Jesus affirmed to the Father, "Your Word is truth" (John 17:17).

5. Scripture is historically reliable. Jesus confirmed, "Just as Jonah was three days and three nights in the belly of the great fish, so will the Son of Man be three days and three nights in the heart of the earth" (Matthew 12:40). He also said, "As were the days of Noah, so will be the coming of the Son of Man. For as in those days before the flood they were eating and drinking, marrying and giving in marriage, until the day when Noah entered the ark, and they were unaware until the flood came and swept them all away, so will be the coming of the Son of Man" (Matthew 24:37-39).

6. Scripture has ultimate supremacy. Jesus told some Jewish leaders, "Why do you break the commandment of God for the sake of your tradition?...For the sake of your tradition you have made void the word of God" (Matthew 15:3,6). Such verses affirm that Scripture is supreme over human tradition.

In view of such facts, you and I can trust every single prophetic statement found in the pages of Scripture. We can be confident that God's words about the future are reliable and true.

A Literal Approach Is Best

In the early eighties, I was one of three or four dozen Dallas Seminary students who worked with a Christian courier company. We delivered various kinds of documents around the Dallas–Fort Worth area.

To do so, we had to learn how to use a map book. By using the index in the back of the map book, we could quickly locate the right map page—and even the right section on the map page—where the street address was located. We were told that as long as we used the map book correctly, we'd never get lost. Whenever I did get lost, it was invariably because I was reading the map book incorrectly.

By analogy, as long as we read the Bible rightly—that is, as long as we interpret it correctly—we'll never get lost in its pages or its teachings. We will understand it the way God intended it to be understood.

I want to briefly address the right way to read the Bible. Once we do this, we'll be better equipped to properly grasp God's revelation about biblical prophecy—especially pertaining to prophetic chronology. We'll also be better able to recognize the folly of such erroneous prophetic ideas as replacement theology* and preterism.†

We begin with the wisdom of taking a literal approach to interpreting Scripture. The word *literal* as used in hermeneutics (the science of interpretation) comes from the Latin *sensus literalis*, which refers to seeking a literal sense of the text as opposed to a nonliteral or allegorical sense of it. It refers to the way any person of normal intelligence would understand the text without using any special keys or codes.

Another way to describe the literal meaning of Scripture is that it embraces the normal, everyday, common understanding of the terms. Words are given the meaning that they normally have in common communication. It is the basic, normal, or plain way of interpreting a passage. But I need to mention a few qualifications.

The Literal Method Does Not Eliminate Figures of Speech

When the Bible speaks of the eye, arms, or wings of God (Psalm 34:15; Isaiah 51:9; Psalm 91:4), these should not be taken as literally

---

* Replacement theology basically argues that the church has replaced Israel in God's plan and that the promises made to Israel are fulfilled in the church.

† The word *preterism* derives from the Latin *preter*, meaning past. In this view, the biblical prophecies in the book of Revelation (especially chapters 6–18) and Christ's Olivet discourse (Matthew 24–25) have already been fulfilled.

true. God does not really have these physical features—He is pure Spirit (John 4:24). Likewise, He cannot literally be a rock (Psalm 42:9), which is material. But we would not know what is *not* literally true of God unless we first know what *is* literally true.

For example, if it were not literally true that God is pure Spirit and infinite, we would not be able to say that certain things attributed to God elsewhere in the Bible are *not* literally true—such as materiality and finitude. When Jesus said "I am the true vine" (John 15:1), the literal method of interpretation does not take this as physically true. Rather, we understand this as a figure of speech—it means that believers derive their spiritual life from Christ, our spiritual vine. It is important to understand all this, for prophetic apocalyptic literature, such as the books of Daniel and Revelation, make heavy use of figures of speech.

Determining when a passage should or should not be taken literally may sometimes be difficult. But certain guidelines are helpful. Briefly, a text should be taken figuratively...

- when it is obviously figurative, as when Jesus said He was a door (John 10:9)
- when the text itself authorizes the figurative sense, as when Paul said he was using an allegory (Galatians 4:24)
- when a literal interpretation would contradict other truths inside or outside the Bible, as when the Bible speaks of the "four corners of the earth" (Revelation 7:1)

In short, as the famous dictum puts it, "When the literal sense makes good sense, seek no other sense lest the result be nonsense." I follow this dictum throughout the rest of the book.

The Literal Method Does Not Eliminate the Use of Symbols

The Bible is filled with symbols. But each symbol is emblematic of something literal.

For example, the book of Revelation contains many symbols that represent literal things. Jesus explained that the seven stars in His right hand were "the seven angels [messengers] to the seven churches" (Revelation 1:20) and that the seven lampstands were the seven churches (1:20). Bowls of incense represent the prayers of the saints (5:8), and "many waters" symbolize "peoples and multitudes and nations and languages" (17:15). Clearly, then, each symbol represents something literal. Textual clues often point us to the literal truth found in a symbol— either in the immediate context or in the broader context of the whole of Scripture.

The Literal Method Does Not Eliminate the Use of Parables

Jesus often used parables that are not to be taken literally. Yet each parable conveys a literal point.

Jesus wanted His parables to be clear to those who were receptive. In fact, He carefully interpreted two of them for the disciples—the parable of the sower (Matthew 13:3-9) and the parable of the weeds (13:24-30). He did this not only so there would be no uncertainty as to their correct meaning but also to show believers how to interpret the other parables. The fact that Christ did not interpret His subsequent parables indicates that He fully expected believers to be able to follow His methodology and understand the literal truths they pointed to.

Six Reasons for a Literal Approach

There are at least six good reasons for adopting a literal interpretation of Scripture (including prophecy).

1. It is the normal way to understand all languages.

2. The greater part of the Bible makes sense when taken literally.

3. This approach will allow for a secondary (allegorical) meaning when demanded by the context.

4. All secondary (or allegorical) meanings actually depend on the literal meaning. We would not know what is not literally true of God unless we first know what is literally true.

5. It is the only sane and safe check on our subjective imaginations.

6. It is the only approach in line with the nature of inspiration (the idea that the words of Scripture are "God-breathed").

Biblical Confirmation of a Literal Interpretation

The biblical text itself provides numerous confirmations of the literal method of interpretation. For example, later biblical texts take earlier ones as literal, as when the creation events in Genesis 1–2 are taken literally by later books (see Exodus 20:10-11). This is likewise the case regarding the creation of Adam and Eve (Matthew 19:6; 1 Timothy 2:13), the fall of Adam and his resulting death (Romans 5:12,14), Noah's flood (Matthew 24:38), and the accounts of Jonah (Matthew 12:40-42), Moses (1 Corinthians 10:2-4,11), and numerous other historical figures.

Further, at Jesus's first coming, He literally fulfilled more than a hundred predictions, including that He would be...

from the seed of a woman (Genesis 3:15)

from the line of Seth (Genesis 4:25)

a descendent of Shem (Genesis 9:26)

the offspring of Abraham (Genesis 12:3)

from the tribe of Judah (Genesis 49:10)

the son of David (Jeremiah 23:5-6)

conceived of a virgin (Isaiah 7:14)

born in Bethlehem (Micah 5:2)

heralded as the Messiah (Isaiah 40:3)

the coming King (Zechariah 9:9)

the sacrificial offering for our sins (Isaiah 53)

pierced in His side at the cross (Zechariah 12:10)

"cut off" (or killed) about AD 33 (Daniel 9:24-26)

resurrected from the dead (Psalm 2; 16)

Note also that by interpreting prophecy literally, Jesus Himself indicated His acceptance of the literal interpretation of the Old Testament (Luke 4:16-21).

Still further, by specifically indicating the presence of parables (Matthew 13:3) or an allegory (Galatians 4:24), the Bible demonstrates that the ordinary meaning is a literal one. And by providing the interpretation of a parable, Jesus revealed that parables have a literal meaning behind them (Matthew 13:18-23).

By rebuking those who did not interpret the resurrection literally, Jesus indicated the literal interpretation of the Old Testament was the correct one (Matthew 22:29-32). Jesus's use of Scripture constitutes one of the most convincing evidences that Scripture ought to be interpreted literally.

The relevance of all this for this book is obvious. A prophet chronology that has any hope of being accurate must follow a literal method of interpreting individual Bible prophecies. The wisdom of this approach will become increasingly evident throughout our study.

You Can Understand Prophetic Scripture

Just as we should use a literal approach in interpreting biblical prophecy, we should use sound interpretive principles for "rightly handling the word of truth" (2 Timothy 2:15). This verse has a depth and richness in the original Greek that does not come across in English translations, as Bible expositor Thomas Constable explains.

> "Handling accurately" (literally, *cutting straight*) is a figure that paints a picture of a workman who is careful and accurate in his work. The Greek word (*orthotomounta*) elsewhere describes a tentmaker who makes straight rather than wavy cuts in his material. It pictures a builder who lays bricks in straight rows and a farmer who plows a straight furrow.[2]

This imagery indicates that just as a craftsman is precise and careful in his work, so must you and I must be when interpreting Scripture. That is why interpretive principles can be so beneficial. Here are six that have guided me through the years.

The Plain Sense

1. When the plain sense makes good sense, seek no other sense lest you end up with nonsense.

I noted this dictum earlier, but it is worth repeating. Bible expositor David Cooper suggests that in view of this dictum, we ought to "take every word at its primary, ordinary, usual, literal meaning, unless the facts of the immediate context, studied in the light of related passages and axiomatic and fundamental truths, indicate clearly otherwise."[3] Likewise, prophecy scholar Arnold Fruchtenbaum suggests that "unless the text indicates clearly that it should be taken symbolically, the passage should be understood literally."[4]

A plain reading of Genesis indicates that when God created Adam in His own rational image, He gave Adam the gift of intelligible speech so he could communicate objectively with the Creator and with other human beings (Genesis 1:26; 11:1,7). Scripture shows that God sovereignly chose to use human language as a medium of communicating revealed truths, often through pronouncements of the prophets. Many times, these men began their messages with "Thus says the LORD" (for example, see Isaiah 7:7; 10:24; 22:15; 28:16; 30:15; 49:22; 51:22; 52:3-4).

If God created language primarily so He could communicate with human beings and so human beings could communicate with each other, He would naturally use language and expect man to use it in its normal and plain sense. This view of language is a prerequisite to understanding not only God's spoken word but also His written Word (Scripture).

Consider the specific promises God has made to Israel, including the land promises in the Abrahamic covenant.[5] The plain meaning of these promises makes perfect sense. There is no good reason to say that such verses will not be fulfilled with Israel but are rather spiritually fulfilled in the modern church—a position held by proponents of replacement theology.

Assumptions

2. Submit all doctrinal assumptions to Scripture.

Our doctrinal opinions should not govern our interpretation of Scripture. Of course, all interpreters are influenced to some degree by personal, theological, denominational, and political prejudices. None of us approaches Scripture with a blank slate. For this reason, our doctrinal opinions must be in harmony with Scripture and subject to correction by it. Only the positions that are compatible with Scripture are legitimate. We must allow the biblical text itself to modify or even completely reshape our presuppositions and beliefs.

For example, many people believe that when the antichrist emerges on the scene, he will be a Muslim. Some of these people seem to have a theological bias in favor of this position because of the recent proliferation of Islamic terrorism.

Testing this position against Scripture, however, reveals significant problems. For one thing, Daniel 9:26 predicts the destruction of Jerusalem in AD 70 but also mentions the antichrist: "The people of the prince who is to come shall destroy the city and the sanctuary." "Prince" refers to the antichrist. The people who destroyed Jerusalem and its temple were the Romans. Since the antichrist is of this people, we can conclude that the antichrist will be a Roman Gentile and not a Muslim. The point is that we must always be willing to test our beliefs against Scripture.

The Biblical Context

3. Pay close attention to the biblical context.

Every word in the Bible is part of a sentence, every sentence is part of a paragraph, every paragraph is part of a book, and every book is part of the whole of Scripture. The interpretation of a specific passage must not contradict the total teaching of Scripture on a point. Individual verses do not exist as isolated fragments, but as parts of a whole. To interpret them properly, we must understand their relationship to the whole and to each other. Scripture interprets Scripture.

As an example of the importance of context, consider Matthew 24:34: "Truly I say to you, this generation will not pass away until all these things take place." Did Jesus mean that *all* end-time prophecies must be fulfilled during the first century, as modern-day preterists hold? I don't think so. Consulting the context indicates that Christ was saying that those people who witness the signs stated *just earlier* in Matthew 24—the abomination of desolation (verse 15), the great tribulation such as has never been seen before (verse 21), the sign of the Son of Man in heaven (verse 30), and the like—will still be alive when the remaining end-time prophecies find fulfillment. The future tribulation period will last seven years (Daniel 9:27; Revelation 11:2), so Jesus is saying the generation alive at the beginning of the tribulation will still be alive at the end of it. Context clears everything up.

Genre

4. Make a correct genre judgment.

The Bible contains a variety of literary genres, each of which has certain peculiar characteristics that we must recognize in order to interpret the text properly. Biblical genres include history (Acts), the dramatic epic (Job), poetry (Psalms), wise sayings (Proverbs), and apocalyptic writings (Daniel and Revelation). Incorrect genre judgments will lead us astray when interpreting Scripture.

A parable should not be treated as history, nor should poetry (which contains many symbols) be treated as a straightforward narrative. For example, the Psalms refer to God as a Rock (Psalm 18:2; 19:14). This should be not be understood literally but seen as a symbol of God's sturdiness—God is our rock-solid foundation. The Psalms often use such metaphors.

The wise interpreter allows his knowledge of genres to control how he approaches each biblical passage. In this way, he can accurately determine what the biblical author was intending to communicate to the reader.

Even though the Bible contains a variety of literary genres and many figures of speech, the biblical authors most often employed literal statements to convey their ideas. Where they use a literal means to express their ideas, the Bible student must employ a corresponding literal approach to explain these ideas. A literal method of interpreting

Scripture gives to each word in the text the same basic meaning it would have in normal, ordinary, customary writing, speaking, or thinking. Without such a method, communication between God and man would be impossible.

To illustrate the importance of genre, we have every indication that the prophetic promise in 1 Thessalonians 4:16-17 should be taken literally.

> For the Lord himself will descend from heaven with a cry of command, with the voice of an archangel, and with the sound of the trumpet of God. And the dead in Christ will rise first. Then we who are alive, who are left, will be caught up together with them in the clouds to meet the Lord in the air, and so we will always be with the Lord.

In other words, there will be a literal rapture. First Thessalonians is an epistle (letter) written by the apostle Paul, and it contains straightforward statements of fact.

On the other hand, in the book of Revelation—an apocalyptic text that includes many symbols—we find that the seven lampstands are the seven churches (Revelation 1:20), the bowls full of incense denote the prayers of the saints (5:8), and the many waters describe "peoples and multitudes and nations and languages" (17:15). Genre distinctions are critical.

The Historical and Cultural Contexts

5. Consult history and culture.

The interpreter of Scripture must step out of his contemporary Western mind-set and into an ancient Jewish mind-set, paying special attention to such things as Jewish marriage rites, burial rites, family practices, farm practices, business practices, the monetary system, methods of warfare, slavery, treatment of captives, use of covenants, and religious practices. Armed with such detailed historical information, interpreting the Bible correctly becomes a much easier task because we better understand the world of the biblical writers.

A thorough historical understanding of Jewish history helps us understand why the antichrist is called the "little horn" (Daniel 8:9). The ancient Jews recognized that animals used their horns as weapons, so the horn eventually came to be seen as a symbol of power and might. As an extension of this symbol, horns in biblical times were sometimes used as emblems of dominion, representing kingdoms and kings, as in the books of Daniel and Revelation (see Daniel 7–8; Revelation 13:1,11; 17:3-16). So the antichrist—as a "little horn"—apparently starts out in a relatively minor way with a localized dominion but eventually attains global dominion (Revelation 13).

Multiple Applications

6. Remember that one passage may apply to more than one event.

Prophetic Scriptures may refer to two events that are separated by a significant time period. These events are nevertheless found in a single passage of Scripture, seemingly blended into one picture, masking the intervening time period. The time gap is not recognized within that particular text, but it becomes evident in consultation with other verses.

This is what we find in certain Old Testament passages about the first and second comings of Jesus Christ. For example, in Zechariah 9:9-10, we read, "Rejoice greatly, O daughter of Zion! Shout aloud, O daughter of Jerusalem! Behold, your king is coming to you; righteous and having salvation is he, humble and mounted on a donkey, on a colt, the foal of a donkey…He shall speak peace to the nations; his rule shall be from sea to sea." This passage speaks both of the first coming (Christ the king mounted on a donkey) and the second coming, which will issue in His universal millennial reign. (See Isaiah 11:1-5 for another example.)

These six interpretive principles will make our efforts to establish a biblical prophetic chronology much easier. Now let's examine specific prophecies in the Scriptures.

Prior to the Tribulation

IN THIS CHAPTER

A Divine Purpose for the Current Age

God has a divine purpose for the current age. I will demonstrate that this purpose relates both to Israel and to the church. God, through Scripture, also provides us with insights regarding the characteristics of the present age. All of this serves as a prelude to specific end-time prophecies about the rapture and the subsequent tribulation period.

God's Purpose for Israel

From the time that Israel rejected Christ in the first century, it has experienced a judicial blindness and hardening as a judgment from God. The apostle Paul put it this way: "I want you to understand this mystery, brothers: a partial hardening has come upon Israel, until the fullness of the Gentiles has come in [that is, until the full number of Gentiles who will be saved have, in fact, become saved]" (Romans 11:25).

The backdrop is that the Jews in Israel had sought a relationship with God not by faith but by works (see Galatians 2:16; 3:2,5,10). Of course, to attain righteousness by observing the law, people must keep the law perfectly (James 2:10), which no person is capable of doing. The Jews stumbled over the "stumbling stone," who is Jesus Christ (Romans 9:31-33). Jesus did not fit their preconceived ideas about the Messiah (Matthew 12:14,24), so they rejected Him. As a result of this rejection of the Messiah, a partial judicial blindness and hardness has come upon Israel. Israel thus lost its favored position before God, so the gospel was preached to the Gentiles to make the Jews jealous that they may be saved (Romans 11:11).

Since that time, Gentiles who place faith in Jesus become members of God's church. Believing Jews also become members of God's church in the current age (see Ephesians 3:3-5,9; Colossians 1:26-27).

The good news is that Israel's hardening and casting off is only temporary. In dire threat at Armageddon, toward the end of the tribulation period, Israel will finally recognize its Messiah and turn to Him for rescue from the invading forces of the antichrist (Zechariah 12:10; see also Romans 10:13-14). A remnant of Israel will be saved (Romans 11:25). (More on all this later in the book.)

God's Purpose for the Church

Today we live in what is called the church age. The universal church is the ever-enlarging body of born-again believers who comprise the body of Christ and over whom He reigns as Lord. Although the members of the church may differ in age, sex, race, wealth, social status, and ability, they are all joined together as one people (Galatians 3:28). All of them share in one Spirit and worship one Lord (Ephesians 4:3-6). This body is comprised of only believers in Christ. The way one becomes a member of this universal body is to simply place faith in Christ (Acts 16:31; Ephesians 2:8-9).

The word *church* is translated from the Greek word *ekklesia*. This Greek word comes from two smaller words. The first is *ek*, which means "out from among." The second is *klesia*, which means "to call." Combining the two words, *ekklesia* means "to call out from among." The church represents those whom God has called out from among the world—both Jews and Gentiles. And those God has called come from all walks of life. All are welcome in Christ's church.

The church has not always existed. Seven key scriptural factors lead us to this conclusion.

1. The church did not exist in Old Testament times. Matthew 16:18 cites Jesus saying that He would build His church. This indicates that the church did not yet exist.

2. This is consistent with the Old Testament text itself, for it does not contain a single reference to the church.

3. In New Testament times, the church is clearly portrayed as distinct from Israel (see Romans 9:6; 1 Corinthians 10:32; Hebrews 12:22-24). Thus, the church is not a mere continuation of Old Testament Israel. It is true that there are some similarities between Israel and the church. Both are part of the people of God, both are part of God's spiritual kingdom, and both participate in the spiritual blessings of the Abrahamic covenant and the new covenant. Beyond this, however, there are notable distinctions. Israel is an earthly political entity (Exodus 19:5-6), but the universal church is the invisible spiritual body of Christ (Ephesians 1:3). Israel was composed of Jews, but the church is composed of both Jews and Gentiles (see Ephesians 2:15). And one becomes a Jew by physical birth, whereas one becomes a member of the church through a spiritual birth (John 3:3).

4. Every single believer in the church age is baptized into the body of Christ (1 Corinthians 12:13), so the church age must have begun on the day of Pentecost, for this is the day when this phenomenon first occurred (Acts 2; 11:15-16).

5. The church is called a mystery that was not revealed to past generations, but was revealed for the first time in the New Testament era. This mystery involved the idea of uniting Jewish and Gentile believers in one spiritual body (see Ephesians 3:3-6,9; Colossians 1:26-27). This lends support to the idea that the church age began on the day of Pentecost. (Individual Jews may become members of the church by faith in Christ in the present age, but God still has a future purpose for Israel. This will become increasingly clear throughout this book.)

6. We are told in Ephesians 1:19-20 that the church is built on the

foundation of Christ's resurrection, meaning that the church could not have existed in Old Testament times.

7. The church is called a "new man" in Ephesians 2:15, meaning it could not have existed in Old Testament times.

We conclude, then, that the genesis of the church was on the day of Pentecost, and that ever since then, we've been living in the church age. This church age will last until the church is raptured off the earth—the dead in Christ will be resurrected, and all living believers on the earth will instantly be translated into their resurrection bodies (1 Thessalonians 4:13-17; 1 Corinthians 15:50-58). I will provide evidence in this book that the rapture takes place prior to the seven-year tribulation period. During the tribulation, God will resume His special dealings with Israel (Daniel 9:26-27).

The Course of the Present Age

As prophecy scholar Thomas Ice demonstrates, Christ's parables in Matthew 13 describe the course of the present age. These parables cover the period of time between Christ's two advents—His first and second comings.[1]

The theological backdrop is that the kingdom had been offered to the Jews by the divine Messiah, Jesus Christ (Matthew 11–12). However, the Jewish leaders not only rejected Jesus but even claimed that His miracles were performed in the power of Satan. This constituted a definitive turning away from Jesus Christ, the Jewish Messiah. This is why a judicial blindness and hardening has come upon Israel as a judgment from God (Romans 11:25).

God's kingdom program was thereby altered—its coming was delayed. (It will be delayed until the future 1000-year millennial kingdom, which follows the second coming of Christ.) In Matthew 13, Jesus revealed what the course of the present age would be like until His second coming. He provided His insights in parables.

The parable of the sower teaches that this age will be characterized by the sowing of the gospel seed onto different kinds of soil (Matthew 13:1-23). This reveals that people will have various responses to the gospel because various forces are opposed to the gospel—including the world, the flesh, and the devil.

The parable of the weeds indicates that the true sowing of the gospel seed will be imitated by a false counter-sowing (Matthew 13:24-30,36-43). Only a judgment following the future tribulation period will separate the wheat (true believers) from the weeds (unbelievers or false believers).

The parable of the mustard seed indicates that God's spiritual kingdom would have an almost imperceptible beginning—hardly even noticeable. But just as a small mustard seed can produce a large plant (it can grow more than 15 feet high), so God's spiritual kingdom would start small but grow to be very large in the world (Matthew 13:31-32).

The parable of the leaven has been interpreted variously by biblical scholars (Matthew 13:33). Most believe that leaven typically represents evil in Scripture (see Matthew 16:12; Mark 8:15; Luke 12:1; 1 Corinthians 5:6-8; Galatians 5:9). For this reason, they conclude that perhaps the parable is teaching that false teaching may emerge and grow exponentially and penetrate Christendom.

The parable of the hidden treasure has also been interpreted variously by biblical scholars (Matthew 13:44). Many believe Jesus was pointing to the incredible value of the true kingdom of heaven as opposed to counterfeit belief systems. Those who truly see its importance will do anything within their power to possess it. They will allow nothing to stand in their way.

Continued Opportunities for Repentance and Conversion

Some may wonder why the second coming of Christ has not already occurred in the present church age. Why doesn't God bring about the end immediately? There is a good answer for this.

Second Peter 3:9 instructs us, "The Lord is not slow to fulfill his promise as some count slowness, but is patient toward you, not wishing that any should perish, but that all should reach repentance." God is patient and is providing plenty of time for people to repent.

This is in keeping with the fact that God has a long track record of showing immense patience before bringing people to judgment (see Joel 2:13; Luke 15:20; Romans 9:22). We should therefore not be surprised that He continues this patience in the present age.

Sadly, despite God's patience and His desire that none will perish, many people will refuse to turn to God and will therefore spend eternity apart from Him (Matthew 25:46). God longs for all to be saved (see 1 Timothy 2:4), but not all will receive God's gift of salvation (see Matthew 7:13-14). That is one of the reasons why so many horrific judgments fall on an unbelieving world during the future tribulation period (Revelation 4–18). The people living on earth during that time will have no excuse!

Israel Reborn as a Nation

The birth of the modern, self-governing nation of Israel in 1948 began the fulfillment of specific Bible prophecies about an international regathering of the Jews in unbelief before the judgments to come during the future tribulation period. This regathering was predicted to take place after centuries of exile in various nations around the world.

In Ezekiel 36:10 God promised the Jewish people, "I will multiply people on you, the whole house of Israel, all of it. The cities shall be inhabited and the wasted places rebuilt." God also promised, "I will take you from the nations and gather you from all the countries and bring you into your own land" (verse 24).

In biblical times, Israel had been in bondage to single nations, such as the Egyptians, the Assyrians, and the Babylonians. And in each case, God delivered them after a time. But never in biblical history have the Israelites been delivered from "all the countries." This event did not find fulfillment until 1948, when Israel finally became a national entity again, and Jews have been streaming back to their homeland ever since. Joel Rosenberg provides this insight:

> Consider the numbers. When Israel declared her independence on May 14, 1948, the country's population stood at only 806,000. Yet by the end of 2005, nearly 7 million people lived in Israel, 5.6 million of whom were Jewish.

Thousands more arrive every year. In 2005 alone, some 19,000 Jews immigrated to Israel. In fact, today more Jews live in the greater Tel Aviv area than in New York City, as many Jews live in Israel as in the United States, and it will not be long before more Jews live in Israel than Jews who do not.[2]

The divine program of restoring Israel has apparently been in progress, even prior to 1948, setting the stage for the future tribulation period. Here are some key dates in recent history:

- 1881–1900: About 30,000 Jews who had been persecuted in Russia moved to Palestine.

- 1897: The goal of establishing a home in Palestine for Jewish people received great impetus when the First Zionist Congress convened in Basel, Switzerland, and adopted Zionism as a program.

- 1904–1914: 32,000 more Jews who had been persecuted in Russia moved to Palestine.

- 1924–1932: 78,000 Polish Jews moved to Palestine.

- 1933–1939: 230,000 Jews who had been persecuted in Germany and central Europe moved to Palestine.

- 1940–1948: 95,000 Jews who had been persecuted in central Europe moved to Palestine. Meanwhile, more than six million Jews were murdered by Adolph Hitler and Nazi Germany.

- 1948: The new state of Israel was born.

- 1967: Israel captured Jerusalem and the West Bank during the Six Day War, which was precipitated by an Arab invasion.[3]

In the vision of dry bones in Ezekiel 37, the Lord miraculously brings scattered bones back together into a skeleton, wraps the skeleton in muscles and tendons and flesh, and breathes life into the body.

There is no doubt that this chapter is speaking about Israel, for we read that "these bones are the whole house of Israel" (verse 11). The chapter portrays Israel as becoming a living, breathing nation, seemingly brought back from the dead.

This means that 1948 is a year to remember. After all, in AD 70 Titus and his Roman warriors destroyed Jerusalem, definitively ending Israel's identity as a political entity (see Luke 21:20). The Jews were dispersed worldwide for many centuries. In 1940, no one could have guessed that within a decade Israel would be a nation again. And yet it happened. Israel achieved statehood in 1948, and Jews have been returning to their homeland ever since.

Biblical prophecy reveals that this newly reborn nation of Israel will become prosperous. God promises, "I will make the fruit of the tree and the increase of the field abundant, that you may never again suffer the disgrace of famine among the nations" (Ezekiel 36:30).

The Stage Is Being Set

The regathering of Jews in Israel is necessary in order for key biblical prophecies about the tribulation period to make sense. The return of the Jews to the land prior to the tribulation period is clearly implied in the peace covenant between the antichrist and the leaders of Israel (Daniel 9:27). The signing of this peace pact will signal the actual beginning of the tribulation period. Note, however, that for such a treaty to make sense, the Jews must be in their own land, and Israel must be a viable political entity. The point is, then, that Israel *must* be regathered to the land before the beginning of the tribulation period. This is what makes the year 1948 so significant from a prophetic standpoint.

We can make the same point in relation to the rebuilding of the Jewish temple that will exist during the tribulation period (see Matthew 24:15-16; 2 Thessalonians 2:4). How could there be a rebuilding of the Jewish temple in Israel unless Israel had been previously reborn as a nation?

A Qualification

I need to be careful to emphasize that Israel at this time still remains in unbelief. But according to Joel 2:28-29, a spiritual awakening in Israel will eventually occur.

Armageddon—the series of battles that occur at the end of the tribulation period—appears to be the historical context in which Israel will finally become converted (Zechariah 12:2–13:1). The restoration of Israel will include the confession of Israel's national sin (Leviticus 26:40-42; Jeremiah 3:11-18; Hosea 5:15), following which Israel will be saved, thereby fulfilling Paul's prophecy in Romans 11:25-27. In dire threat at Armageddon, Israel will plead for their newly found Messiah to return and deliver them. "They shall mourn for Him, as one mourns for an only child" (Zechariah 12:10; Matthew 23:37-39; see also Isaiah 53:1-9), and their deliverance will surely come (see Romans 10:13-14). Israel's leaders will have finally realized the reason why the tribulation has fallen on them—perhaps because the Holy Spirit will enlighten their understanding of Scripture, or because of the testimony of the 144,000 Jewish evangelists (Revelation 7), or because of the testimony of the two prophetic witnesses (Revelation 11).

Later, in the millennial kingdom, which follows the second coming of Christ, Israel will experience a full possession of the promised land and the reestablishment of the Davidic throne. It will be a time of physical and spiritual blessing, the basis of which is the new covenant (Jeremiah 31:31-34).

Apostasy Increases

The word *apostasy* comes from the Greek word *apostasia*, which means "falling away." The word refers to a falling away from the truth. It depicts a determined, willful defection from the faith or an abandonment of the faith.

Judas Iscariot's betrayal of Jesus for 30 pieces of silver is a classic example of apostasy and its effects (see Matthew 26:14-25,47-57; 27:3-10). He fell away from the truth, perhaps for financial reasons. Later, in remorse, Judas hanged himself, after which his body fell headlong and "burst open in the middle and all his bowels gushed out" (Acts 1:18).

Hymenaeus and Alexander experienced a shipwreck of their faith and apparently engaged in blasphemy (1 Timothy 1:19-20). Demas turned away from the apostle Paul because of his love for the present world (2 Timothy 4:10).

Whether people are enticed by money or the love of the world or something else, they can be enticed away from their commitment to the Lord. And the consequences are always severe—even deadly. The apostles often warned of the danger of apostasy (Hebrews 6:4-8; 10:26-27).

Apostasy also occurred in Old Testament times among the Israelites (Joshua 22:22; 2 Chronicles 33:19; Jeremiah 2:19; 5:6). As a result of their apostasy, they went into exile (the northern kingdom was exiled by Assyria in 722 BC, and the southern kingdom was exiled by Babylon in 597–581 BC).

Paul warned church elders that following his death, false teachers would emerge who would seek to lead church members into apostasy: "I know that after my departure fierce wolves will come in among you, not sparing the flock, and from among your own selves will arise men speaking twisted things, to draw away the disciples after them" (Acts 20:29-30).

Scripture tells us that there will be an increase of apostasy in the end times. For example, 1 Timothy 4:1-2 warns, "The Spirit expressly says that in later times some will depart from the faith by devoting themselves to deceitful spirits and teachings of demons, through the insincerity of liars whose consciences are seared."

Many of the cults and false religions that pepper our land today emerged out of the Christian church. The leaders of these groups received alleged revelations from angels—which we know to be fallen angels, or demons. Mormonism is a classic example. It was founded by Joseph Smith after he received a revelation from the alleged angel Moroni. Another example is Islam, which is based on alleged revelations that the angel Gabriel brought to Muhammad.

Moreover, 2 Timothy 4:3-4 offers this warning: "The time is coming when people will not endure sound teaching, but having itching ears they will accumulate for themselves teachers to suit their own passions, and will turn away from listening to the truth and wander off into myths." Who can doubt that these words describe the very days in which we live? Channel-surfing on television in the evening, you will come across examples of numerous such false teachers espousing doctrines that appeal to people's passions, such as the health and wealth gospel.

Second Timothy 3:1-8 provides some specifics regarding end-times apostasy:

> Understand this, that in the last days there will come times of difficulty. For people will be lovers of self, lovers of money, proud, arrogant, abusive, disobedient to their parents, ungrateful, unholy, heartless, unappeasable, slanderous, without self-control, brutal, not loving good, treacherous, reckless, swollen with conceit, lovers of pleasure rather than lovers of God, having the appearance of godliness, but denying its power. Avoid such people. For among them are those who creep into households and capture weak women, burdened with sins and led astray by various passions, always learning and never able to arrive at a knowledge of the truth. Just as Jannes and Jambres opposed Moses, so these men also oppose the truth, men corrupted in mind and disqualified regarding the faith.

Scripture reveals that apostasy is often encouraged by false teachers (Galatians 2:4) and escalates during times of trial (Luke 8:13). This is prophetically significant, for false teachers and severe trials will proliferate in the future tribulation period.

Scripture is clear that apostasy will rise to a fever pitch during the future tribulation period. In 2 Thessalonians 2:3 we read, "Let no one deceive you in any way. For that day will not come, unless the rebellion comes first." Many believe this refers to a rebellion against the truth.

Matthew 24:9-12, a passage speaking about the tribulation period, includes many of these themes: "Many will fall away...many false prophets will arise and lead many astray...the love of many will grow cold."

Sobering days lie ahead.

The United States Weakens

Is America mentioned in Bible prophecy? Many have thought so. Some prophecy enthusiasts have suggested interpretations that are speculative and far-fetched. Others have taken a more reasoned approach.

The Bible is clear that the United States of Europe—the revived Roman Empire that will be headed by the antichrist—will be the political and economic superpower in the end times (see Daniel 2; 7). This being the case, many prophecy scholars believe the United States will progressively weaken by the time the tribulation period begins. I personally believe this is a strong possibility. And there are a number of scenarios that might explain how it could happen.

Moral Implosion

The continued moral and spiritual degeneration of the United States could cause it to implode. Many statistics show the trouble this country is in morally and spiritually. At present, four out of five adults—some 83 percent—say they are concerned about the moral condition of the United States. If this country's moral fiber continues to erode, its demise is only a matter of time.

Because of the high level of immorality in this country, God may bring judgment upon it. Christian leaders have been warning about this possibility for decades, but their warnings often fall on deaf ears, just as the prophets were often ignored during Old Testament times.

Scripture reveals that God is absolutely sovereign (Psalm 50:1; 66:7; 93:1; Proverbs 19:21; Isaiah 14:24; 46:10), and in His sovereignty He blesses nations that submit to Him and brings down nations that rebel against Him. In the book of Job we read, "He makes nations great, and he destroys them; he enlarges nations, and leads them away" (Job 12:23). Daniel 2:20-21 tells us that God "removes kings and sets up kings." In view of such scriptural facts, is America ripe for judgment? We have cause for concern.

- God is absolutely sovereign over the nations.
- Both the Old and New Testaments affirm that God is a God of judgment.
- America is in a free fall, plummeting morally and spiritually, with no repentance in sight.
- We must therefore ask whether God might sovereignly judge America in the end times for turning away from Him.

I hate to say so, but I think this is a real possibility. Those who doubt this should consult what the apostle Paul says in Romans 1:18-28:

> For the wrath of God is revealed from heaven against all ungodliness and unrighteousness of men, who by their unrighteousness suppress the truth. For what can be known about God is plain to them, because God has shown it to them. For his invisible attributes, namely, his eternal power and divine nature, have been clearly perceived, ever since the creation of the world, in the things that have been made. So they are without excuse. For although they knew God, they did not honor him as God or give thanks to him, but they became futile in their thinking, and their foolish hearts were darkened...
>
> Therefore God gave them up in the lusts of their hearts to impurity, to the dishonoring of their bodies among themselves, because they exchanged the truth about God for a lie and worshiped and served the creature rather than the Creator, who is blessed forever! Amen.
>
> For this reason God gave them up to dishonorable passions. For their women exchanged natural relations for those that are contrary to nature; and the men likewise gave up natural relations with women and were consumed with passion for one another, men committing shameless acts with men and receiving in themselves the due penalty for their error.

> And since they did not see fit to acknowledge God, God gave
> them up to a debased mind to do what ought not to be done.

If this passage tells us anything, it is that when a nation continues to willfully reject God and His Word, turning its back on His moral requirements, God eventually reveals His wrath against that nation. God has a long track record of wrath against ungodly nations. This passage reveals that one way God reveals His wrath is by allowing the people of that nation to experience the full brunt of the ravaging consequences of their sin.

Many great nations have risen and fallen throughout human history. In each case, the nation had no expectation of its impending demise. Indeed, those who lived in these nations probably believed that their nation could never fall. "Anthropology tells us that many of the fallen civilizations in history also thought they were superior to their neighbors and forebears. Few of their citizens could have imagined their society would suddenly collapse."[4] But the harsh reality of documented history is that great nations do fall—and they fall hard.

How about a small dose of real history? The Babylonian Empire lasted less than a century. The Persian Empire capitulated after about two centuries. Greece waned in less than three centuries. The mighty Roman Empire held out for nine centuries. The citizens of these empires probably thought their nations would last forever, but each empire suffered a gross moral decline, and God rendered appropriate judgment.

Here is a question to ponder: If what we are witnessing in America today—pornography, premarital sex, extramarital sex, widespread homosexuality, same-sex marriages, abortions, drinking, drugs, divorce, the disintegration of the family unit, and the like—were taking place in ancient Babylon, would you think that Babylon was ripe for judgment? I think so! The problem today is that many in our country have become desensitized to moral issues because immorality is so rampant. That is a dangerous state to be in, for God's patience will not last forever.

Nuclear Detonation

Another possibility is that the United States could be weakened by a nuclear detonation on its soil. The United States stands a good chance of being attacked with nuclear weapons at some point in the not-too-distant future. Government advisors are presently saying that a nuclear attack on US soil within the next ten years is more likely than not.

Granted, the entire United States would not be likely to be destroyed by a nuclear attack. But if one major city—such as New York City, Los Angeles, Chicago, or Houston—were destroyed, the effect would be absolutely devastating on the already fragile, debt-ridden US economy.

Electromagnetic Pulse (EMP) Attack

Yet another possibility is that the United States could be incapacitated by an electromagnetic pulse (EMP) attack. This possibility is documented in a report issued in 2004 by a blue-ribbon commission created by Congress called "Commission to Assess the Threat to the United States from Electromagnetic Pulse Attack." Based on this report, a number of highly respected government officials lament that the technology is now here to bring America's way of life to an end.

The commission found that a single nuclear weapon, delivered by a missile to an altitude of a few hundred miles over the United States, would yield catastrophic damage to the nation. Such a missile could easily be launched from a freighter off the coast of the United States. The commission explained that the higher the altitude of the weapon's detonation, the larger the affected geographic area would be. At a height of 300 miles, the entire continental United States would be exposed, along with parts of Canada and Mexico.

The commission warned that the electromagnetic pulse produced by such a weapon would be likely to severely damage electrical power systems, electronics, and information systems—all of which Americans depend on. At high risk would be electronic control, the infrastructures for handling electric power, sensors and protective systems of all kinds, computers, cell phones, telecommunications, transportation, fuel and energy, banking and finance, emergency services, and even food and water. Anything electrical is at risk.

The consequences of an EMP attack would be especially harmful to American society today because the infrastructure of our society—civilian and military—virtually runs on electricity and electronic components. The commission estimated that "months to years" would be required to fully recover from such an attack.

A major EMP attack could potentially lead to starvation and disease. Expert testimony presented before Congress indicated that an EMP attack could reduce the United States to a pre-industrial-age capacity in terms of transportation options and the ability to provide food and water to the population. Instead of cars, buses, and trains, people would be reduced to using bikes, horses, and buggies.

An Overdependence on Oil

In my book *The Coming Oil Storm* (Harvest House Publishers, 2010), I noted yet another possibility. Perhaps the United States will weaken due to its gross overdependence on oil. Experts are now telling us that a progressive lessening in the oil supply will progressively weaken the economy of our oil-driven society. At present, our entire infrastructure (including transportation, manufacturing, farming, and much more) depends on a sustained supply of oil. Once the oil supply begins to dwindle—an imminent possibility, according to oil company presidents, geologists, and government leaders—the years to follow could bring shortages that could cause global recession or worse. The United States would be hit especially hard because we are the world's largest consumer of oil.

The Rapture of the Church

One final possibility is that the rapture will catastrophically weaken the United States—more so than it will affect most other nations—because of the high concentration of Christians in this country.

Following the moment of the rapture, many business leaders and their employees will no longer show up for work; bills, mortgages, and other loans will go unpaid; law enforcement officers and other first responders will not be available; and the stock market will likely crash as panic ensues. This and much more will follow the rapture.

A Composite Catastrophe

Any of these scenarios, and especially a combination of them, could greatly weaken the United States. This seems likely to happen because prophecy reveals that in the end times, the balance of power will shift toward the United States of Europe—that is, the revived Roman Empire, which will be led by the antichrist. I will demonstrate later in the book that the United States will likely become an ally with the revived Roman Empire.

3

The Rapture

The Church Will Be Raptured

The rapture is that glorious event in which the dead in Christ will be resurrected, living Christians will be instantly translated into their resurrection bodies, and both groups will be caught up to meet Christ in the air and taken back to heaven (John 14:1-3; 1 Corinthians 15:51-54; 1 Thessalonians 4:13-17). This means that one generation of Christians will never pass through death's door. They will be alive on earth in their mortal bodies, and suddenly, in an instant, they will be with Christ in their immortal bodies. What a moment that will be!

The Bible offers several clues that the rapture will take place prior to the tribulation period. This means the church will not go through the judgments prophesied in Revelation 4–18. This view seems to be most consistent with a literal interpretation of biblical prophecy.

In Revelation 3:10, for example, Jesus promises the church in Philadelphia, "I will keep you from the hour of trial that is coming on the whole world, to try those who dwell on the earth." Notice the definite article (*the*) before the word *hour* in this verse. This indicates that a specific and distinctive time period is in view, not just any "hour of trial" in church history. The context clearly points to the future seven-year tribulation, which is described in detail in Revelation 6–19. This is the hour of trial from which the church is to be kept.

This verse reveals that the church saints will be kept from the actual hour of testing, not just the testing itself. If the Lord meant to communicate that He would preserve them in the midst of the testing itself, He would have omitted the words *the hour* and simply said, "I will keep you from the testing."

The Greek text supports this view. The Greek preposition *ek* (translated *from*) carries the idea of separation from something. This means that believers will be kept from the hour of testing in the sense that they will be completely separated from it by being raptured before the period even begins. Renald Showers comments on this in his book *Maranatha: Our Lord Come!*

> The language in Jesus' reference to this future period of worldwide testing implied that it was well-known to the church saints. It was well-known because both Old and New Testament Scriptures, written years before Revelation, foretold this unique, future period of testing or Tribulation, which would take place prior to the coming of the Messiah to rule the world in the Messianic Age or Millennium (Isa. 2:10-21; Dan. 12:1; Zeph. 1:14-18; Mt. 24:4-31).[1]

Notice that Revelation 3:10 promises only that *church* saints will be kept out of this hour of trial coming upon the entire earth. Those who become believers during the hour of trial itself (those we might call tribulation saints) will go through tribulation. Arnold Fruchtenbaum explains this in his book *The Footsteps of the Messiah*.

> Throughout the Tribulation, saints are being killed on a massive scale (Rev. 6:9-11; 11:7; 12:11; 13:7, 15; 14:13; 17:6; 18:24). If these saints are *Church* saints, they are not being kept safe and Revelation 3:10 is meaningless. Only if

Church saints and *Tribulation* saints are kept distinct does the promise of Revelation 3:10 make any sense.[2]

In keeping with the idea that the church will be raptured before this time of tribulation begins, no Old Testament passage on the tribulation mentions the church (Deuteronomy 4:29-30; Jeremiah 30:4-11; Daniel 8:24-27; 12:1-2). Likewise, no New Testament passage on the tribulation mentions the church (Matthew 13:30,39-42,48-50; 24:15-31; 1 Thessalonians 1:9-10; 5:4-9; 2 Thessalonians 2:1-11; Revelation 4–18). The church's complete absence would seem to indicate that it is not on earth during the tribulation.

Further, a pretribulational rapture best explains the massive apostasy that engulfs the world following the removal of "the restrainer"— apparently the Holy Spirit (2 Thessalonians 2:3-7). The Holy Spirit indwells all believers (John 14:16; 1 Corinthians 3:17), so He will essentially be removed when the church is raptured, thus making possible the eruption of apostasy.

Still further, Scripture assures us that the church is not appointed to wrath (Romans 5:9; 1 Thessalonians 5:9). This means the church cannot go through the great day of wrath—the tribulation period (Revelation 6:17; 14:10,19; 15:1,7; 16:1).

First Thessalonians 1:10 explicitly states that Jesus "delivers us from the wrath to come." The Greek word translated *delivers* means "to draw or snatch out to oneself, to rescue, to save, to preserve." Indeed, Greek scholar Marvin Vincent, author of *Word Studies in the New Testament*, says the verb literally means "to draw to one's self" and almost invariably refers to deliverance from some evil or danger or enemy.[3] This clearly seems to be referring to the rapture of the church prior to the beginning of the tribulation period.

In fact, this definition of the Greek word in 1 Thessalonians 1:10 reminds us of the description of the rapture in 1 Thessalonians 4:16-17.

> For the Lord himself will descend from heaven with a cry of command, with the voice of an archangel, and with the sound of the trumpet of God. And the dead in Christ will rise first. Then we who are alive, who are left, will be caught

up together with them in the clouds to meet the Lord in
the air, and so we will always be with the Lord.

The phrase "caught up" here literally means "snatched up or taken
away." Moreover, the Greek preposition *ek* ("from") is used in this verse,
just as it is used in Revelation 3:10. As we have seen, the term carries the
idea of "separation from." Believers will be delivered from this wrath by
being completely separated from it, which requires the rapture.

Throughout Scripture, God protects His people before judgment
falls (see 2 Peter 2:5-9). Enoch was transferred to heaven before the
judgment of the flood. Noah and his family were in the ark before
the floodgates were opened. Lot was taken out of Sodom before judgment was poured out on Sodom and Gomorrah. The firstborn among
the Hebrews in Egypt were sheltered by the blood of the Paschal lamb
before judgment fell. The spies were safely out of Jericho and Rahab
was secured before judgment fell on Jericho. So too will the church be
secured safely (by means of the rapture) before judgment falls in the
tribulation period.

We find parallels between the apostle Paul's description of the rapture in 1 Thessalonians 4:16-18 and his words in 1 Thessalonians 5:10-11:
"[Christ] died for us so that whether we are awake or asleep we might
live with him. Therefore encourage one another and build one another
up, just as you are doing." Note these similarities:

1 THESSALONIANS 4:16-18	1 THESSALONIANS 5:10-11
the dead in Christ	asleep
we who are alive	awake
Encourage one another with these words.	Encourage one another and build one another up.

We can thus infer that both passages refer to the rapture. There are
also parallels between 1 Thessalonians 4:13-18 and Jesus's description
of the rapture in John 14:2-3. For example:

- John 14:3 depicts Jesus descending from heaven to earth.

Likewise, 1 Thessalonians 4:16 says Christ "will descend from heaven."

- In John 14:3 Jesus says to believers, "I will come again and will take you to myself." First Thessalonians 4:17 reveals the believers will be "caught up" to Christ.

- In John 14:3, Jesus promises, "I will…take you to myself, that where I am, you may be also." First Thessalonians 4:17 affirms that believers "will always be with the Lord."

- Jesus shares His words in John 14:1 so that His followers' hearts will not be troubled. Likewise, Paul shares the information in 1 Thessalonians 4:13,18 to minimize grief and bring encouragement.

These similarities make clear that both passages are referring to the same event—the rapture of the church. The scriptural evidence reveals that it takes place prior to the tribulation.

This is confirmed in the fact that the rapture involves Christ coming *for* His saints in the air prior to the tribulation, whereas at the second coming He will come *with* His saints to the earth to reign for a thousand years (Revelation 19; 20:1-6). The fact that Christ comes with His holy ones (redeemed believers) at the second coming presumes they have been previously raptured. (He cannot come *with* them until He has first come *for* them.)

The Rapture—a Mystery

A mystery, in the biblical sense, is a truth that cannot be discerned simply by human investigation, but rather requires special revelation from God. Generally, this word refers to a truth that was unknown to people living in Old Testament times but was revealed to humankind by God during Jesus's and the apostles' ministries (Matthew 13:17; Colossians 1:26). This is illustrated in a key verse about the rapture of the church.

> Behold! I tell you a mystery. We shall not all sleep, but we shall all be changed, in a moment, in the twinkling of

an eye, at the last trumpet. For the trumpet will sound, and the dead will be raised imperishable, and we shall be changed. For this perishable body must put on the imperishable, and this mortal body must put on immortality. When the perishable puts on the imperishable, and the mortal puts on immortality, then shall come to pass the saying that is written: "Death is swallowed up in victory." "O death, where is your victory? O death, where is your sting?" (1 Corinthians 15:51-55).

The rapture of the church is a mystery because it had never been revealed in Old Testament times. It was revealed for the first time in the New Testament.

The Twinkling of an Eye

In 1 Corinthians 15:51-52 the apostle Paul describes the rapture as occurring "in the twinkling of an eye." This phrase is Paul's way of demonstrating how brief the moment of the rapture will be. The fluttering of an eyelid, the blinking of an eye, is exceedingly fast.

This means the bodily transformation that living believers will experience at the rapture will be nearly instantaneous. One moment they will be on earth in mortal bodies, and the next moment they will meet Christ in the clouds, instantly transformed into their glorified resurrection bodies.

The Voice of an Archangel

The apostle Paul tells us that the rapture of the church will follow "a cry of command, with the voice of an archangel" (1 Thessalonians 4:16). Scholars debate what is meant by this phrase. Some suggest that perhaps Jesus will issue the shout with an archangel-like voice. However, it seems more natural to the text to interpret this shout as actually coming from the voice of the archangel himself.

Scripture reveals that at the second coming, the Lord Jesus shall be "revealed from heaven with his mighty angels" (2 Thessalonians 1:7). If the angels accompany Christ at the second coming, surely the archangel Michael will be included. And if the angels accompany Jesus at the second coming, there is no reason to assume they will not also accompany Him seven years earlier at the rapture. After all, angels are often portrayed as being heavily involved in end-time events (see Revelation 5:11; 7:1-2,11; 8:2,4,6; 9:14-15; 10:10; 12:7,9; 14:10; 15:1,6-8; 16:1; 17:1; 21:9,12).

The Bridegroom and His Bride

Scripture portrays Christ as the bridegroom (John 3:29) and the church as His bride (Revelation 19:7). The backdrop to this imagery is rooted in Hebrew weddings, which had three phases. First, the marriage was legally consummated by the parents of the bride and groom, after which the groom went to prepare a place to live in his father's house. Next, the bridegroom came to claim his bride. Finally, there was a marriage supper, which could last several days. All three of these phases are seen in Christ's relationship to the church, the bride of Christ.

1. As individuals living during the church age come to salvation, under the Father's loving and sovereign hand, they become a part of the bride of Christ (the church). Meanwhile, Christ, the Bridegroom, is in heaven, preparing a place for the bride of Christ to live in His Father's house.

2. The Bridegroom (Jesus Christ) comes to claim His bride (at the rapture) and take her to heaven, where He has prepared a place for her (John 14:1-3). The actual marriage takes place in heaven prior to the second coming (Revelation 19:6-16).

3. The marriage supper of the Lamb will follow the second coming, apparently taking place during a 75-day interim period between the second coming of Christ and the beginning of the millennial kingdom (see Daniel 12:11; compare with Matthew 22:1-14; 25:1-13). (More on this interim period later in the book.)

We can see other parallels as well. Just as ancient Jewish grooms paid a purchase price to establish the marriage covenant, so Jesus paid a purchase price for the church (1 Corinthians 6:19-20). Also, just as a Jewish bride was declared sanctified or set apart in waiting for her groom, so the church is declared sanctified and set apart for Christ the Bridegroom (Ephesians 5:25-27; 1 Corinthians 1:2; 6:11; Hebrews 10:10; 13:12). And just as a Jewish bride was unaware of the exact time her groom would come for her, so the church is unaware of the exact time that Jesus the Bridegroom will come, though it is an imminent event.

The Blessed Hope

The term "blessed hope" in Scripture is a general reference to the rapture of the church. This event is blessed in the sense that it brings blessedness to believers. The term carries the idea of joyous anticipation. Believers can hardly wait for it to happen!

We read of this in Titus 2:13, where Paul says we Christians are "waiting for our blessed hope, the appearing of the glory of our great God and Savior Jesus Christ." At this momentous event, the dead in Christ will be resurrected and believers still alive on earth will be instantly translated into their resurrection bodies (see Romans 8:22-23; 1 Corinthians 15:51-58; Philippians 3:20-21; 1 Thessalonians 4:13-18; 1 John 3:2-3). These bodies will never again be subject to sickness, pain, and death. As we continue to pass through this fallen world as pilgrims, we are empowered by this magnificent hope.

The Rapture Is Imminent

The term *imminent* literally means "ready to take place" or "impending." The New Testament teaches that the rapture is imminent—that is, nothing must be prophetically fulfilled before the rapture can occur (see 1 Corinthians 1:7; 16:22; Philippians 3:20; 4:5; 1 Thessalonians 1:10; Titus 2:13; Hebrews 9:28; 1 Peter 1:13; Jude 21). The rapture is a signless event that can occur at any moment. This is in contrast to the second coming of Christ, which is preceded by many events that transpire during the seven-year tribulation period (see Revelation 4–18).

The imminence of the rapture is certainly implied in the apostle Paul's words in Romans 13:11-12: "You know the time, that the hour has come for you to wake from sleep. For salvation is nearer to us now than when we first believed. The night is far gone; the day is at hand. So then let us cast off the works of darkness and put on the armor of light."

The word *salvation* in this context must be eschatological, referring to the rapture, for Paul describes it as a specific future event. At the end of each day, the Christian is that much closer to the rapture.

The imminence of the rapture is also implied in James 5:7-9.

> Be patient, therefore, brothers, until the coming of the Lord. See how the farmer waits for the precious fruit of the earth, being patient about it, until it receives the early and the late rains. You also, be patient. Establish your hearts, for the coming of the Lord is at hand. Do not grumble against one another, brothers, so that you may not be judged; behold, the Judge is standing at the door.

Scripture does say some believers will be alive during the tribulation period (for example, Revelation 6:9-11). But these people become believers sometime after the rapture. Perhaps they become convinced of the truth of Christianity after witnessing millions of Christians supernaturally vanish off the planet at the rapture. Or perhaps they become believers as a result of the ministry of the 144,000 Jewish evangelists introduced in Revelation 7 (who themselves come to faith in Christ after the rapture). Or they may have become believers as a result of the miraculous ministry of the two witnesses of Revelation 11, prophets who apparently have the same powers as Moses and Elijah. As well, Christian literature will be left behind after the rapture, and many may come to faith after reading such books.

The imminent coming of Christ at the rapture should have an incredible practical effect on the lives of individual Christians and the church as a whole.

> The fact that the glorified, holy Son of God could step through the door of heaven at any moment is intended by God to be the most pressing, incessant motivation for holy living and aggressive ministry (including missions, evangelism, and Bible teaching) and the greatest cure for lethargy and apathy. It should make a difference in every Christian's values, actions, priorities, and goals.[4]

Pretribulationism Is the Preferred View

I am thoroughly convinced that the pretribulational view of the rapture, outlined above, is correct. However, some Christians hold to different views. These include posttribulationism, midtribulationism, the partial rapture theory, and the prewrath view. I will briefly explain what these views are and why I believe they are incorrect.

Posttribulationism

The posttribulational view, expressed in the writings of George Eldon Ladd, Robert Gundry, and others, is the view that Christ will rapture the church after the tribulation period at the second coming of Christ. This means the church will go through the time of judgment prophesied in the book of Revelation, but believers will be kept from Satan's wrath during the tribulation (Revelation 3:10). Pretribulationists (such as myself) respond, however, that Revelation 3:10 indicates believers will be saved out of or separated from (Greek: *ek*) the actual time period of the tribulation.

Posttribulationists argue that Revelation 20:4-6 proves that all believers will be resurrected at the end of the tribulation period. Pretribulationists respond, however, that in context, only those people who become believers during the tribulation and then die will be resurrected at the end of the tribulation period. Believers who live prior to the tribulation will be resurrected earlier at the rapture (1 Thessalonians 4:13-17).

Posttribulationists rebut that saints are seen on earth during the tribulation, and this must therefore mean the rapture has not yet occurred. Again, pretribulationists grant that there will be saints who live during the tribulation period (for example, Revelation 6:9-11). But these people become believers sometime after the rapture.

Posttribulationists counter by citing Matthew 24:37-40. In this passage, set in the context of the second coming of Christ, we are told that "two men will be in the field; one will be taken and the other left." Pretribulationists respond, however, that the context indicates that those who are taken are taken not in the rapture but are taken away in judgment to be punished (see Luke 17:37). This is not the rapture.

Some posttribulationists try to bolster their view by the claim that pretribulationism emerged late in church history, finding its origin in John Nelson Darby (1800–1882), who allegedly got it from Edward Irving (1792–1834). Thus, the majority of church history knew nothing of this novel view. Pretribulationists respond that the key issue is what the Bible actually teaches, not when the belief first emerged.

Besides, some in the early church held to false doctrines, such as baptismal regeneration. Just because a doctrine was held early in church history does not mean it is correct. Conversely, just because a doctrine developed late in church history does not mean it is incorrect.

Many believe that with the process of doctrinal development through the centuries, eschatology would naturally become a focus later in church history. Besides, many throughout church history—as early as the first century—have held to the doctrine of the imminent return of Christ, a key feature of pretribulationism.

The truth is, the pretribulational view is most consistent with a literal approach to biblical prophecy. And the precedent has been set for the reliability of a literal approach. After all, the messianic prophecies dealing with the first coming of Christ (more than 100 of them) were fulfilled literally!

Midtribulationism

Midtribulationism—the view that Christ will rapture the church in the middle of the tribulation period—has been taught by such proponents as Gleason Archer (1916–2004), J. Oliver Buswell (1895–1977), and Merrill Tenney (1904–1985). The two witnesses of Revelation 11, who are caught up to heaven after they are resurrected, are believed to be representative of the church. Pretribulationists respond, however, that there is virtually no indication in the context that these witnesses represent the church.

Midtribulational proponents argue that the church will be delivered from wrath (1 Thessalonians 5:9), which, they argue, is in the second half of the tribulation, but not from tribulation in the first half. Pretribulationists point out, however, that the entire tribulation period is characterized by wrath (Zephaniah 1:15,18; 1 Thessalonians

1:10; Revelation 6:17; 14:7,10; 19:2), so it makes more sense to say the church is delivered from the entire seven-year period (Revelation 3:10).

Midtribulational proponents also argue that because the rapture occurs at the last trumpet (1 Thessalonians 4:16-17), and because the seventh trumpet sounds in the middle of the tribulation (Revelation 11:15-19), the rapture must occur during the middle of the tribulation. Pretribulationists, however, interpret Revelation 11:15 as showing that the seventh trumpet sounds at the end of the tribulation. Besides, the seventh trumpet is unrelated to the rapture but rather deals with judgment.

The Partial Rapture View

The partial rapture view, expressed in the writings of Witness Lee (1905–1997), is based on the parable of the ten virgins. Five virgins were prepared, and five were unprepared (Matthew 25:1-13). This is interpreted to mean that only faithful and watchful Christians will be raptured. Unfaithful Christians will be left behind to suffer through the tribulation period.

Pretribulationists respond, however, that this verse has nothing to do with the rapture. Those virgins who were unprepared apparently refer to people living during the tribulation period who are unprepared for Christ's second coming (seven years after the rapture). Besides, Scripture indicates when people believe, they are saved and will participate in the rapture. Moreover, the Spirit's baptism places all believers in Christ's body (1 Corinthians 12:13), so all believers will be raptured (1 Thessalonians 4:16-17). The partial rapture view does not fit the facts of biblical prophecy.

Prewrath View

The prewrath view, represented by Robert Van Kampen and Marvin Rosenthal, argues that the rapture occurs toward the end of the tribulation period before the great wrath of God falls. It is argued that the Bible indicates the church will not experience the wrath of God (2 Thessalonians 1:5-10). Since the word *wrath* does not appear in Revelation until after the sixth seal, God's wrath must not be poured out until the seventh seal (Revelation 6:12–8:1). Therefore, the rapture must take place between the sixth and seventh seals.

Pretribulationists raise a number of problems with this view, not the least of which is that God's wrath is poured out on the earth prior to the seventh seal (Zephaniah 1:15,18; 1 Thessalonians 1:10; Revelation 6:17; 14:7,10; 19:2). Scripture pictures the seven seals as a sequence, all coming from the same ultimate source—God (Revelation 6; 8). This sequence features divine judgments that increase in intensity with each new seal. Both human beings and warfare are seen to be instruments of God's wrath during the first six seals. Even the unsaved who experience this wrath recognize it specifically as the "wrath of the Lamb" (Revelation 6:15-16), who Himself opens each seal that causes each respective judgment (see Revelation 6:1,3,5,7,9,12; 8:1). Besides, all the seal judgments are complete in the first half of the tribulation period, not toward the end of the tribulation period, as this view suggests. The prewrath view does not fit the facts of biblical prophecy.

We conclude that the rapture of the church is best placed prior to the tribulation period. This view is most consistent with a literal interpretation of biblical prophecy.

4

The Results of the Rapture

The Restrainer Is Removed

"The mystery of lawlessness is already at work. Only he who now restrains it will do so until he is out of the way. And then the lawless one will be revealed" (2 Thessalonians 2:7-8). This verse indicates that the lawless one (the antichrist) cannot be revealed until the one who restrains is taken out of the way.

But who is this restrainer? And how does the restrainer relate to the mystery of lawlessness? What is the mystery of lawlessness? *The Bible Knowledge Commentary* offers this explanation:

> A mystery in the New Testament is a new truth previously unknown before its revelation in the present dispensation. In this case the mystery is the revelation of a future climax of lawlessness in the world. Then and now a movement against divine law directed by Satan was and is operative. But it is being restrained somewhat, and this restraining will continue until the time appointed for revealing the man of sin and the climax of lawlessness.[1]

The "man of sin" (2 Thessalonians 2:3 NKJV) is the antichrist. He will embody sin and will promote sin as it has never been promoted before. Everything about him will be rooted in sin.

Of course, this aspect of biblical prophecy would be much easier if Scripture precisely identified who (or what) the restrainer is. But for reasons known only to God, this information is not provided to us in Scripture. However, as will become clear below, we can logically infer who the restrainer is.

First, however, let's review some inadequate views.

Rome

Some of the church fathers believed that the restrainer mentioned in 2 Thessalonians 2:7-8 was the Roman Empire. They believed the restraining power was embodied in the person of the Roman emperor.

These church fathers suggested that the apostle Paul was purposefully vague about the identity of the restrainer. After all, if he explicitly identified the restrainer as Rome and his epistle fell into the hands of Roman authorities, his statement about Rome being removed might be viewed as seditious.

This understanding of the restrainer may have made some sense to people living during those days, but from our vantage point today we can see multiple problems with it. Foundationally, the Roman Empire fell from power in the fifth century AD, and the antichrist is yet to be revealed. This means that the restrainer of 2 Thessalonians 2:7-8 cannot be the Roman Empire.

There is another explanation for Paul's vagueness that makes good sense. Paul had already spoken to the Thessalonians verbally about the restrainer. Thus, Paul's brief allusion to it in 2 Thessalonians 2 would have been readily understood by them without him having to explain it in detail again.

Another thorny problem for the Rome view is that the antichrist will not only be a powerful figure himself, exercising authority over the whole world, but will also be empowered by Satan. Thus, many interpreters say the restrainer must be powerful enough to stand against

Satan. They suggest that no human being or human government has the power to restrain Satan's work.

Further, Scripture reveals that the antichrist will rule over a revived Roman Empire (Daniel 2; 7). It thus hardly makes sense to say that the Roman Empire—itself a bastion of false religion—would restrain the coming of the antichrist.

Human Government

In a similar view, human government in general is said to restrain the antichrist. The idea here is that "restraint through the rule of law [by the government] is the opposite of the man of sin and the mystery of lawlessness."[2] In other words, lawlessness is restrained by the enforcement of law by the government. In this view, the antichrist will one day overthrow human government so that he can work his lawless will in the world.

Perhaps the most cogent argument for this view comes from prophecy scholar Arnold Fruchtenbaum in his book *The Footsteps of the Messiah*.

> The task of restraining evil was given to human government under the Noahic Covenant in Genesis 9:1-17, and this basic doctrinal truth was reiterated by Paul in Romans 13:1-7. On one hand, human government is even now restraining lawlessness. On the other hand, the government of the last of the three kings will restrain the Antichrist, the lawless one, until the middle of the Tribulation.[3]

Fruchtenbaum is referring to Daniel 7:7, which speaks of the rise of the antichrist.

> Behold, a fourth beast, terrifying and dreadful and exceedingly strong. It had great iron teeth; it devoured and broke in pieces and stamped what was left with its feet. It was different from all the beasts that were before it, and it had ten horns. I considered the horns, and behold, there came up among them another horn, a little one, before which three

of the first horns were plucked up by the roots. And behold, in this horn were eyes like the eyes of a man, and a mouth speaking great things.

This wild imagery refers to the Roman Empire. Rome already existed in ancient days, but it fell apart in the fifth century AD. It will be revived, however, in the end times, apparently comprised of ten nations ruled by ten kings (ten horns). An eleventh horn—a little one (the antichrist)—starts out apparently in an insignificant way but grows powerful enough to uproot three of the existing horns (kings) who apparently resist his rise. He eventually comes into absolute power and dominance over this revived Roman Empire. Fruchtenbaum offers this interpretation:

> It is only when the last of these three kings has been killed, leading to complete submission by the other seven kings, that the Antichrist will be free to take over full global dictatorship…Consequently, the last restrainer of the Antichrist will be the last of the three kings and the government which he represents.[4]

It is certainly possible that Fruchtenbaum is right. If there is a weakness to the view, it relates to whether human beings—who make up human government—are strong enough to stand against the antichrist, who will be energized by Satan. Indeed, Satan is more powerful than humans by a large measure, so some Bible interpreters reject the possibility of any form of human government restraining him. One scholar notes, "It would seem that a person is required to restrain a person, and a supernatural one to restrain this man of lawlessness who is motivated by Satan himself."[5]

Some Bible expositors also point out that both Scripture and modern empirical evidence reveal that not all human governments restrain sin—some actually encourage it. So it may be unrealistic to say that the restrainer is human government, especially during the future tribulation period, when lawlessness will prevail. But this view still remains a possibility.

The Holy Spirit

Many theologians believe that only one person—the omnipotent God—is powerful enough to restrain Satan. For this reason, they interpret the restrainer as being the Holy Spirit who indwells the church. This view was held by many in the early church, including Theodoret, Theodore of Mopsuestia, and Chrysostom.[6]

Bible expositor Thomas Constable is representative of more modern scholars. "The Holy Spirit of God is the only Person with sufficient [supernatural] power to do this restraining...The removal of the Restrainer at the time of the Rapture must obviously precede the day of the Lord."[7]

In keeping with this, 1 John 4:4 tells us, "He who is in you is greater than he who is in the world." "He who is in" Christians is the Holy Spirit, who is more powerful than "he who is in the world"—that is, the devil.

The Popular Bible Prophecy Commentary draws support for this view from the grammar of 2 Thessalonians 2.

> The word "restrain" (Greek, *katecho*, "to hold down") in both verses 6 and 7 is a present active participle, but in verse 6 it appears in the neuter gender ("what restrains") while in verse 7 it is in the masculine ("he who restrains, holds down"). Such usage also occurs in reference to the Spirit of God. The Greek word for "spirit," *pneuma*, is a neuter gender word, but the masculine pronoun is used when referring to the person of the Holy Spirit.[8]

The Greek word translated *restrain* carries the idea, "to hold back from action, to keep under control, to deprive of physical liberty, as by shackling."[9] This is what the Holy Spirit does in our day in preventing the antichrist from arising.

The Holy Spirit's restraining of the lawless one (the antichrist) is in keeping with His broader work of restraining sin in the world. Prophecy expert Mark Hitchcock notes, "The Holy Spirit is spoken of in Scripture as restraining sin and evil in the world (see Genesis 6:3) and in the heart of the believer (see Galatians 5:16-17)."[10] Mal Couch likewise tells us, "By divine providence, and by all the evidence of the Scriptures, the Holy Spirit characteristically restrains and strives against sin (Genesis 6:3). The Spirit presently abides in the world in a special way in this age through the church."[11] Once this special work of the Holy Spirit is removed, the antichrist will be manifest.

Taken out of the Way at the Rapture

When the rapture occurs, the church—the universal body of believers in Christ from the day of Pentecost right on up to the present (Ephesians 1:3; 2:5; see also Acts 1:5; 1 Corinthians 12:13)—will be caught up to be with Christ in the air. This church is indwelt by the Holy Spirit. First Corinthians 3:16 tells us, "Do you not know that you are God's temple and that God's Spirit dwells in you?" First Corinthians 6:19 tells us, "Do you not know that your body is a temple of the Holy Spirit within you, whom you have from God?" First Corinthians 12:13 tells us, "In one Spirit we were all baptized into one body—Jews or Greeks, slaves or free—and all were made to drink of one Spirit" (see also 1 John 3:24).

This means that if the church is taken off the earth at the rapture (John 14:1-3; 1 Corinthians 15:51-54; 1 Thessalonians 4:13-17), the Holy Spirit will be "out of the way." This removal of the Holy Spirit's restraint allows the antichrist, energized by Satan, to come into power during the tribulation period.

The Holy Spirit in the Tribulation

If the Holy Spirit is taken out of the way at the rapture, will He still be active on earth during the tribulation period? I believe He will. So does Bible scholar John Phillips.

> The church age is a parenthesis in God's dealing with the world. The church, injected supernaturally into history at Pentecost and supernaturally maintained throughout the age by the baptizing, indwelling, and filling works of the Holy Spirit, will be supernaturally removed when this age is over. What is to be removed then is the Holy Spirit's

mighty working through the church. Until that happens, Satan cannot bring his plans to a head...

After the rapture of the church, the Holy Spirit will continue His work in bringing people to salvation, but He will no longer baptize them into the mystical body of Christ, the church, nor will He actively hinder Satan from bringing His schemes to fruition. Once Satan has achieved his centuries-long goal, Christ will return and demolish the whole thing![12]

Bible scholar Paul Feinberg agrees.

There seems to be abundant evidence that the Holy Spirit will be active in the earth during the tribulation period. He will empower His witnesses (Mark 13:11). Evangelism will be more effective than it has ever been (Matt. 24:14; Rev. 7:9-14). It is reasonable to assume that as satanic activity increases, so will the activity of the Holy Spirit.[13]

So the Holy Spirit will still be active on earth during the tribulation period. But His work will not be identical to that of the present age.

Christians Are Resurrected (Glorified)

The evidence that Jesus Christ was physically resurrected from the dead is overwhelming (Matthew 28:1-15; Mark 16:1-11; Luke 24:1-12; John 20:1-18; Acts 1:3; 1 Corinthians 15:1-4; Colossians 1:18; Revelation 1:5,18). Once He was resurrected, many witnesses came forward to attest that it happened (Acts 2:32; 3:15; 10:39-40; 1 Corinthians 15:3-8; see also John 20:24-29).

The wondrous fact that now lies before us is that Jesus's resurrection ensures our own resurrection from the dead. Recall Jesus's words to Martha following the death of Lazarus: "I am the resurrection and the life. Whoever believes in me, though he die, yet shall he live, and everyone who lives and believes in me shall never die" (John 11:25-26). To prove His authority to make such statements, Jesus promptly raised Lazarus from the dead!

Jesus had made a similar affirmation before. "This is the will of him who sent me, that I shall lose nothing of all that he has given me, but raise it up on the last day. For this is the will of my Father, that everyone who looks on the Son and believes in him should have eternal life, and I will raise him up on the last day" (John 6:39-40).

Because of what Jesus Himself accomplished on our behalf, we too shall be resurrected from the dead. We can rest in the quiet assurance that even though our mortal bodies may pass away in death, turning to dust in the grave, they will be gloriously raised, never again to grow old and die.

> What are death, the grave, and decomposition in the presence of such power as this?…Millions that have been moldering in the dust for thousands of years shall spring up in a moment into life, immortality and eternal glory, at the voice of that blessed One.[14]

Raised Imperishable, Glorious, and Powerful

This wondrous resurrection from the dead will take place at the rapture of the church. In an instant—in the twinkling of an eye—dead believers will be raised from the dead. Even better, at that same rapture, the bodies of living Christians will be instantly transformed into resurrection bodies, and we will all meet the Lord in the air (1 Thessalonians 4:13-17). Never again will we be subject to the frailties of our weak, mortal bodies.

In 1 Corinthians 15:42-43, the apostle Paul says this of the resurrection body: "What is sown is perishable; what is raised is imperishable. It is sown in dishonor; it is raised in glory. It is sown in weakness; it is raised in power." What a forceful statement this is of the nature of our future resurrection bodies.

Paul here graphically illustrates the contrasts between our present earthly bodies and our future resurrection bodies. The reference to sowing is probably a metaphorical reference to burial. Just as one sows a seed in the ground, so the mortal body is "sown" in the sense that it is buried in the ground. When our bodies are placed in the grave, they decompose and return to dust.

The exciting thing is that the resurrection body is raised out of the ground. Paul notes that our present bodies are perishable. The seeds of disease and death are ever upon them. Fighting off dangerous infections is a constant struggle. We often get sick, and all of us eventually die. It is just a question of time. Our new resurrection bodies, however, will be raised imperishable. All liability to disease and death will be forever gone. Never again will we have to worry about infections or passing away.

What does Paul mean when he says our present bodies are "sown in dishonor"? Any way you look at it, having your lifeless corpse lowered into the ground and having dirt heaped on it is anything but honorable. We may try to bring honor to a funeral service by dressing our dead loved ones in their best clothes, purchasing a fancy casket, bringing in beautiful flowers, and offering glowing eulogies. And we should do all of these things. But underlying it all is the fact that death—despite our efforts to camouflage it—is intrinsically dishonoring. After all, man was created to live forever with God, not to die and be buried in the ground.

Our new bodies, by contrast, will be utterly glorious. No dishonor here. Our new bodies will never again be subject to aging, decay, or death. Never again will our bodies be buried in the ground. How great it will be!

Paul also notes that our present bodies are characterized by weakness. From the moment we are born, "our outer nature is wasting away" (2 Corinthians 4:16; see also 1:8-9). Vitality decreases, illness comes, and then old age follows with its wrinkles and decrepitude. Eventually, in old age, we may become utterly incapacitated, not able to move around and do the simplest of tasks.

By contrast, our resurrection body will be one of great power. "Our new body, like our Lord's, will be characterized by power. Sleep will not be necessary to relieve weariness or recoup spent energy. Our abilities will be enlarged and we will throw off the limitations of which we are so conscious in life on earth."[15] Never again will we tire or become weak or incapacitated. Words truly seem inadequate to describe the incredible differences between our present bodies (those that will be "sown" in the earth) and our future resurrection bodies.

Strong like a Building

The apostle Paul compared our present earthly bodies to tents and our permanent resurrection bodies to buildings (2 Corinthians 5:1-4). Paul was speaking in terms that his listeners would have readily understood. After all, the temporary tabernacle of Israel's wanderings in the wilderness (a giant tentlike structure) was eventually replaced with a permanent building in the promised land (the temple) when Solomon was king. In like manner, the temporary "tent" (or body) in which believers now dwell will be replaced on the day of the rapture with an eternal, immortal, imperishable body (see 1 Corinthians 15:42,53-54). One commentator paraphrased Paul's words this way:

> Don't take your physical situation too seriously. Your body is fine to camp out in for a while, but before long, the tent will begin to sag; a stake or two will be lost along the way; seams will begin to tear…Our Father is so good to gently remind us every time we look in the mirror that we're rushing toward eternity. Paul was one who truly understood that his body was only a temporary dwelling.[16]

Paul's statement in 2 Corinthians 5:4 (NIV) is particularly relevant: "For while we are in this tent [of our present mortal body], we groan and are burdened, because we do not wish to be unclothed [without a body] but to be clothed instead with our heavenly dwelling [resurrection body], so that what is mortal [our earthly body] may be swallowed up by life [resurrection]." Paul here indicates that being "unclothed"—that is, being without a physical body as a result of death—is a state of incompletion and for him carries a sense of nakedness. Even though departing to be with Christ in a disembodied state is far better than life on earth (Philippians 1:21-23), Paul's true yearning was to be "clothed" with a physically resurrected body (see 2 Corinthians 5:6-8). That yearning will be fully satisfied on that future day of resurrection at the rapture.

Meanwhile, as Paul said, "we groan." Why? Because our bodies are burdened by sin, sickness, sorrow, and death. Commentator Albert Barnes explains it this way: "The sense is…that the body is subjected to so many pains, and to so much suffering, as to make us earnestly desire to be invested with that body which shall be free from all susceptibility to suffering."[17] Or, more to the point, "We groan because our 'tents' are showing signs of use, because our bodies are wearing out."[18]

The Holy Spirit: A Deposit

In 2 Corinthians 5:5, the apostle Paul affirmed that God has given us the Holy Spirit as a deposit of what is to come in the afterlife. Paul had just referred to our earthly bodies as tents and our future resurrection bodies as buildings (verses 1-3). While still existing in our mortal bodies, however, Paul says we groan (verse 4). Moreover, Paul said, we ideally prefer to immediately receive resurrection bodies instead of temporarily becoming disembodied spirits—despite the fact that being a disembodied spirit with Christ in heaven is far better than our present lives on earth (Philippians 1:23).

In this context, Paul added that God has given us the Holy Spirit as a deposit of what is yet to come. The Greek word translated *deposit* was used among the Greeks to refer to a pledge that guaranteed final possession of an item. It was sometimes used of an engagement ring, which acted as a guarantee that the marriage would take place. The Holy Spirit is a deposit in the sense that His presence in our lives guarantees our eventual total transformation and glorification into the likeness of Christ's glorified resurrection body (see Philippians 3:21). The Holy Spirit in us is a guarantee of what is to come.

This helps us to maintain an eternal perspective. Our present bodies truly are wearing down. They've been infected by the fatal disease of sin. One day, they will simply cease functioning (they will fall down like a flimsy tent). By contrast, our resurrection bodies in heaven will never again wear down, never again get sick, and never again die (they will be as solid and sturdy as a building). "There will be no blind eyes in heaven. No withered arms or legs in heaven. No pain or agony there. Tears will be gone. Death will be gone. Separation will be gone. This will be the ultimate healing. Then and only then, we will be free at last."[19]

Physical Resurrection Bodies

Our resurrection bodies will be physical. How do we know this to be so? We know it because Jesus was physically resurrected from the dead, and Scripture promises that our resurrection bodies will be like His resurrection body. How do we know that Jesus's resurrection body was physical?

- The body was missing from the tomb (Matthew 28; Mark 16; Luke 24; John 20).

- It retained the crucifixion scars (Luke 24:39-40; John 20:27).

- It was composed of flesh and bones (Luke 24:39).

- People touched it (Matthew 28:9; John 20:27-28).

- It was visible (Matthew 28:17).

- Christ ate food after His resurrection (Luke 24:30,42-43; John 21:12-13; Acts 1:4).

We know our resurrection bodies will be the same, for Christ "will transform our lowly bodies so that they will be like his glorious body" (Philippians 3:21 NIV). John likewise said, "Dear friends, now we are children of God, and what we will be has not yet been made known. But we know that when Christ appears, we shall be like him, for we shall see him as he is" (1 John 3:2 NIV). These body upgrades will be awesome!

5

The Church with Christ in Heaven

The Judgment Seat of Christ

All believers will one day stand before the judgment seat of Christ (the *bema*) (Romans 14:8-10; 1 Corinthians 3:11-15; 9:24-27). At that time each believer's life will be examined in regard to deeds done while in the body. Personal motives and intents of the heart will also be weighed.

The idea of a judgment seat goes back to the athletic games of Paul's day. After the games concluded, a dignitary took his seat on an elevated throne in the arena. One by one the winning athletes came up to the throne to receive a reward—usually a wreath of leaves, a victor's crown. In the case of Christians, each of us will stand before Christ the Judge and receive (or lose) rewards.

Christ's judgment of us will not be in a corporate setting—like a big class being praised or scolded by a teacher. Rather, it will be individual and personal. "We will all stand before the judgment seat of God" (Romans 14:10). Each of us will be judged on an individual basis.

This judgment has nothing to do with whether the Christian will remain saved. Those who have placed faith in Christ *are* saved, and nothing threatens that. Believers are eternally secure in their salvation (John 10:28-30; Romans 8:29-39; Ephesians 1:13; 4:30; Hebrews 7:25). This judgment rather has to do with the reception or loss of rewards. First Corinthians 3:12-15 describes this judgment this way:

> Now if anyone builds on the foundation with gold, silver, precious stones, wood, hay, straw—each one's work will become manifest, for the Day will disclose it, because it will be revealed by fire, and the fire will test what sort of work each one has done. If the work that anyone has built on the foundation survives, he will receive a reward. If anyone's work is burned up, he will suffer loss, though he himself will be saved, but only as through fire.

Notice Paul lists the materials according to their combustibility. Precious metals and stones do not burn. Wood does, and hay and straw even more so.

This is also the order of their usefulness for building. A house constructed with solid materials such as stones and metals will stand and last a long time. But a house made of hay or straw could easily topple or burn.

What do these building materials represent? Gold, silver, and costly stones may refer to things we accomplish by the power of the Holy Spirit, things we do with Christ-honoring motives and godly obedience. Wood, hay, and straw, however, refer to perishable things and may represent carnal attitudes, sinful motives, pride-filled actions, and selfish ambition.

Fire in Scripture often symbolizes the holiness of God (Leviticus 1:8; Hebrews 12:29) and His judgment upon that which His holiness has condemned (Genesis 19:24; Mark 9:43-48). At the judgment seat, God will examine our works and test them against the fire of His holiness. If our works are built with good materials—precious metals and stones—our works will stand. But if our works are built with less valuable materials—wood, hay, or straw—they will burn up.

Perhaps the figure is intended to communicate that those works performed with a view to glorifying God are the works that will stand. Those works performed with a view to glorifying self, performed in the flesh, are those that will be burned up.

The Possibility of Shame

Some believers at the judgment seat of Christ may experience a sense of deprivation and suffer some degree of forfeiture and shame. Indeed, certain rewards may be forfeited that otherwise might have been received, and this will involve a sense of loss. Second John 8 thus warns us, "Watch yourselves, so that you may not lose what we have worked for, but may win a full reward" (compare with 1 John 2:28).

We must keep all this in perspective, however. Christ's coming for us at the rapture and the prospect of living eternally with Him is something that should give each of us joy. And our joy will last for all eternity. Some people will fare better than others at the judgment seat of Christ, but all of us will be in heaven, and we will all dwell face-to-face with Christ forever!

The Scope of the Judgment

The Christian's judgment will focus on his personal stewardship of the gifts, talents, opportunities, and responsibilities given to him in this life. The very character of each Christian's life and service will be laid bare under the unerring and omniscient vision of Christ, whose eyes are like a flame of fire (Revelation 1:14).

Actions. Numerous Scripture verses reveal that each of our actions will be judged before the Lord. The psalmist said to the Lord, "You will render to a man according to his work" (Psalm 62:12; see also Matthew 16:27). In Ephesians 6:7-8 we read that "whatever good anyone does, this he will receive back from the Lord."

Thoughts. At Christ's judgment seat, He will scrutinize more than just our actions. He will also judge our thoughts. In Jeremiah 17:10 God said, "I the LORD search the heart and test the mind, to give every man according to his ways, according to the fruit of his deeds." The Lord "will bring to light the things now hidden in darkness and will disclose the purposes of the heart" (1 Corinthians 4:5). The Lord is the one "who searches mind and heart" (Revelation 2:23).

Words. Finally, the scope of the believer's judgment will include all the words he has spoken. Christ said that "people will give account for every careless word they speak" (Matthew 12:35-37). This is an important aspect of judgment, for tremendous damage can be done through the human tongue (see James 3:1-12).

The Judgment Follows the Rapture

Scripture reveals that this judgment will take place immediately after Christ meets the saints in the air (at the rapture) and takes them back to heaven. No Bible verse explicitly states this, but a number of factors lead us to this conclusion.

First, many biblical scholars believe that the 24 elders in heaven that are mentioned in Revelation 4:4,10 represent believers. They are portrayed as already having received their crowns in heaven at the very start of the tribulation period (see 2 Timothy 4:8; James 1:12; 1 Peter 5:4; Revelation 2:10). The fact that they are dressed in white may be significant, for these same words were previously used of believers in the churches (see Revelation 3:5,18). All this would seem to indicate that the judgment of believers has already taken place sometime following the rapture.

In keeping with this, Scripture often describes the rewards Christians receive at the judgment as crowns that we wear. In fact, there are a number of different crowns that symbolize the various spheres of achievement and award in the Christian life.

- The crown of life is given to those who persevere under trial and especially to those who suffer to the point of death (James 1:12; Revelation 2:10).

- The crown of glory is given to those who faithfully and sacrificially minister God's Word to the flock (1 Peter 5:4).

- The imperishable crown is given to those who win the race of temperance and self-control (1 Corinthians 9:25).

- The crown of righteousness is given to those who long for the second coming of Christ (2 Timothy 4:8).

Revelation 4:10 informs us that the 24 elders (apparently representing believers in heaven) cast their crowns before the throne of God in an act of worship and adoration. It seems clear that this heavenly scene takes place sometime after the rapture.

Moreover, when the bride of Christ (the corporate body of Christians) returns to earth with Christ at the second coming, she is adorned in "fine linen, bright and pure," which we are told represents "the righteous deeds of the saints" (Revelation 19:8). Clearly believers in the body of Christ have already been judged, which lends credence to the idea that the judgment seat of Christ follows the rapture.

The Marriage of the Lamb

Scripture describes the relationship between Christ and the church as a marriage. Christ is the Bridegroom, and the church is the bride. Jesus Christ, the Lamb, frequently referred to Himself as a bridegroom (see Matthew 9:15; 22:2-14; 25:1-13; Mark 2:19-20; Luke 5:34-35; 14:15-24; John 3:29). The church is regarded as a virgin bride awaiting the coming of her heavenly bridegroom (2 Corinthians 11:2). While she waits, she keeps herself pure, unstained from the world.

> "Let us rejoice and exult and give him the glory, for the marriage of the Lamb has come, and his Bride has made herself ready; it was granted her to clothe herself with fine linen, bright and pure"—for the fine linen is the righteous deeds of the saints. And the angel said to me, "Write this: Blessed are those who are invited to the marriage supper of the Lamb." And he said to me, "These are the true words of God" (Revelation 19:7-9).

In chapter 3, we noted three aspects of Hebrew weddings that are relevant to this discussion: The bride was betrothed to the bridegroom, the bridegroom came to claim his bride, and the marriage feast was celebrated. All three of these aspects are seen in Christ's relationship to the church, the bride of Christ.

1. As individuals living during the church age come to salvation, they become a part of the church, the bride of Christ, which is betrothed to Christ, the Bridegroom. If you trust in Christ anytime during the church age, you are in!

2. The Bridegroom (Jesus Christ) then comes to claim His bride at the rapture, at which time He takes His bride to heaven, the Father's house, where He has prepared a place to live (John 14:1-3). The actual marriage takes place in heaven sometime after the church has been raptured and prior to the second coming (Revelation 19:11-16). Arnold Fruchtenbaum, in his book *The Footsteps of the Messiah*, suggests that the marriage ceremony necessarily takes place after the judgment seat of Christ.

> The marriage ceremony takes place in heaven and involves the church. That it must take place after the judgment seat of Messiah is evident from [Revelation 19:8], for the bride is viewed as being dressed in white linen, which is the righteous acts of the saints. This means that all the wood, hay, and stubble has been burned away and all the gold, silver, and precious stones have been purified. Thus, following the rapture of the church in which the Bridegroom brings the bride with Him to His home, and following the judgment seat of Messiah which results in the bride having the white linen garments, the wedding ceremony takes place.[1]

The bride is dressed beautifully. As Bible expositor Thomas Constable notes, "God graciously enabled her to clothe herself in fine linen... 'Bright' indicates divine glory, and 'clean' reflects purity...This is dress appropriate for God's presence.[2] John MacArthur adds, "Such dazzling garments were worn earlier in Revelation by angels (15:6), and will be the clothing of the armies of heaven (made up of both angels and the redeemed saints) that accompany Christ when He returns to earth (v. 14)."[3]

3. The marriage supper of the Lamb takes place on earth sometime later, apparently during the 75-day interval between the end of the tribulation period and the beginning of the millennial kingdom. (More on this later in the book.)

The Invasion of Israel

Israel at Peace in the Land

Some 2600 years ago, the prophet Ezekiel prophesied that the Jews would be regathered from many nations to the land of Israel in the end times (Ezekiel 36–37). He then predicted an all-out invasion of Israel by a massive northern assault force composed of Russia, Iran, Turkey, Sudan, Libya, and others. The goal of the assault force will be to utterly obliterate the Jews. With the sheer size of this assault force, Israel will have virtually no chance of defending itself.

Before I address this invasion in detail, I want to emphasize that a precondition for this end-times invasion is that Israel must be living in security and at rest. Ezekiel makes this quite clear in his prophecy about the invaders.

> After many days you will be mustered. In the latter years you will go against the land that is restored from war, the land whose people were gathered from many peoples upon the mountains of Israel, which had been a continual waste.

Its people were brought out from the peoples and now
dwell securely, all of them (Ezekiel 38:8).

We are also told that this invasion force will move against Israel, a
"land of unwalled villages...the quiet people who dwell securely, all of
them dwelling without walls, and having no bars or gates" (38:11). This
invasion by the northern military coalition simply cannot take place
until this state of security exists for Israel. But what brings about this
sense of security? There are at least two possible interpretive scenarios.

A Present Reality

Some prophecy scholars and teachers believe that Israel is already
in a state of relative security. Joel Rosenberg, for example, believes that
Israel's present level of security is based on multiple factors, including
the fall of Saddam Hussein's regime, the death of Yasser Arafat, Israel's
peace treaties with some nations in the Middle East, the withdrawal of
the Syrians from Lebanon, and Israel's well-equipped army, first-rate
air force, effective missile-defense system, strong economy, and strong
relationship with the United States.

> Note that the Hebrew prophet does not go so far as to say
> there will be a comprehensive peace treaty between Israel
> and all of her neighbors, or that all or even most hostili-
> ties in the Middle East will have ceased. But he does make
> it clear that in "the last days" (Ezekiel 38:16 NASB) before
> the Russian-Iranian attack, the Jewish people are "living
> securely" in "the land that is restored from the sword" (Eze-
> kiel 38:8 NASB).[1]

Rosenberg thus feels that present conditions in Israel fulfill the
spirit of Ezekiel's prophecy. This view is also held by prophecy scholar
Arnold Fruchtenbaum.

> This is not a security due to a state of peace, but a security
> due to confidence in their own strength. This...is a good
> description of Israel today. The Israeli army has fought four
> major wars since its founding and won them swiftly each

time. Today Israel is secure, confident that her army can repel any invasion from the Arab states. Hence, Israel is dwelling securely.[2]

A Future Reality

Other Christians take a different view. They say that since Israel became a nation in 1948, it has had to stay on high alert because of the danger from all its Arab and Muslim neighbors. Israel has never been able to let her guard down. Because of the constant conflict and tension in the Middle East, one Western leader after another has tried to broker a peace deal for the region. Stability in the oil-producing Middle East and Persian Gulf area is a high priority for the entire world.

In view of this, some believe that Israel will experience true security only when the leader of a revived Roman Empire—a European superstate—signs a peace pact or covenant with Israel, an event that will officially begin the tribulation period (Daniel 9:27). This leader—the antichrist—will seemingly accomplish the impossible, solving the Middle East peace puzzle. These Bible interpreters suggest that from the moment of the signing of the covenant on through the next three and a half years, Israel will enjoy a heightened sense of security, and this security will be backed by the military might of the most powerful political leader in the world.

Chronological Options

Both of these views are entirely possible, and both sides of the debate are supported by good Bible scholars. In terms of the chronology of end-times biblical prophecy, these scenarios unfold a bit differently.

In the first scenario, Israel is presently in a state of security, and this sense of security does not depend on the antichrist's signing of the covenant with Israel. Seen in this light, the invasion of the northern military coalition could take place at any time before the tribulation period begins.

In the second scenario, however, Israel's state of security depends on the antichrist's signing of the covenant with Israel. This means that the invasion cannot take place until the tribulation period begins—perhaps right after the tribulation period begins.

My Assessment

My assessment is that Israel is already in a state of relative security and that the invasion will likely take place sometime after the rapture but before the beginning of the tribulation period. Prophecy scholar Thomas Ice agrees and suggests that the invasion "will be during the interval of days, weeks, months, or years between the rapture and the start of the seven-year tribulation."[3] Here are five arguments that support this view.

1. The world will likely be in a state of chaos following the rapture. The rapture will have a devastating effect on the United States, which has a heavy population of Christians. Russia and her Muslim allies may well seize the moment, considering this the ideal time to launch a massive attack against Israel, which had been protected by the United States.

2. Once God destroys the Russian and Muslim invaders prior to the tribulation period, the door may be open for the rise of the antichrist as the leader of a European superstate—the revived Roman Empire.

> I have always thought that one of the strengths of this view is the way in which it could set the stage for the biblical scenario of the tribulation. If the tribulation is closely preceded by a failed regional invasion of Israel (by Russia and her Muslim allies), then this would remove much of the Russian and Muslim influence currently in the world today and allow a Euro-centric orientation to arise.[4]

3. With the Muslim invaders having already been destroyed prior to the beginning of the tribulation period, the antichrist could easily sign a peace pact with Israel (Daniel 9:27), guaranteeing that Israel will be protected. In other words, Israel will be easier to protect if the Muslim forces are already out of the picture.

4. This scenario may account for Israel's ability to construct the

Jewish temple on the temple mount in Jerusalem. With Muslim forces destroyed, Muslim resistance will be greatly minimized.

5. If the invasion takes place after the rapture, and the rapture takes place at least three and a half years prior to the beginning of the tribulation period, the weapons used in the invasion could be completely burned for seven years (Ezekiel 39:9-10) prior to the midpoint of the tribulation, when Israel takes flight from Jerusalem (Matthew 24:15-21). Therefore, a significant lapse of time may separate the rapture from the beginning of the tribulation.

Israel Invaded by a Northern Military Coalition

Now we turn to the invasion itself, prophesied in Ezekiel 38–39. The goal of the northern assault force will be to utterly obliterate the Jews. These are the nations that will be included in the invasion:

- Rosh, which likely refers to modern Russia, to the uttermost north of Israel.

- Magog, which probably includes the former southern Soviet republics of Kazakhstan, Kyrgyzstan, Uzbekistan, Turkmenistan, Tajikistan, and possibly even northern parts of modern Afghanistan.

- Meshech and Tubal, which refer to the area south of the Black and Caspian Seas—modern Turkey.

- Persia, which became Iran in 1935 and the Islamic Republic of Iran in 1979.

- Ethiopia, or modern-day Sudan.

- Put, or modern-day Libya. The term may also include Algeria and Tunisia.

- Gomer, which apparently refers to part of modern-day Turkey.

- Beth-togarmah, which also apparently refers to modern-day Turkey, though it may also include Azerbaijan and Armenia.

This unique alignment of nations has never occurred in the past but is occurring today, which lends credence to the idea that we are living in the end times.

An alliance between many of these nations may not necessarily have made good sense in Ezekiel's day because they are not even located near each other and because Islam did not yet exist. However, such an alliance makes great sense today because the nations that make up the coalition are predominantly Muslim. That in itself is more than enough reason for them to unify in attacking Israel—especially considering current Islamic hatred for Israel.

When Does the Invasion Occur?

In the previous chapter, I pointed out that Israel must be living in a state of security when this invasion occurs (Ezekiel 38:8,11). I suggested that such a state now exists and that the invasion will likely take place sometime after the rapture but prior to the beginning of the tribulation period—perhaps even three and a half years prior to the beginning of the tribulation period (see Ezekiel 39:9-10).

Some scholars claim that Ezekiel 38–39 may refer to an invasion that has already taken place. Here are six reasons why I believe this view is wrong.

1. Israel has never been invaded on the scale of what is described in Ezekiel 38–39. Nor has an invasion into Israel involved the specific nations mentioned in the passage. This prophecy has not been fulfilled yet, so its fulfillment must yet be future.

2. Ezekiel was clear that the things of which he spoke would be fulfilled "in the latter years" (Ezekiel 38:8) and "in the latter days" (verse 16). Such phrases point to the end times.

3. The unique alignment of nations as described in Ezekiel 38–39 has never occurred in the past but is apparently occurring today.

4. Ezekiel affirmed that the invasion would occur after Israel was regathered from all around the earth—"gathered from many peoples" (Ezekiel 38:8,12)—to a land that had been a wasteland. Certainly there were occasions in Israel's history where the Jews were held in bondage. For example, they were held in bondage in Egypt. They went into

captivity in Assyria, as well as in Babylon. But in each of these cases, their deliverance involved being set free from a single nation, not many nations around the world. The only regathering of Jews from "many peoples" around the world in Israel's history is that which is occurring in modern days (especially since 1948, when Israel achieved statehood).

5. Since chapters 36–37 are apparently being literally fulfilled (a regathering from "many peoples"), we can reasonably and consistently assume that chapters 38–39 will likewise be literally fulfilled. This is in keeping with the well-established precedent of biblical prophecies throughout the Old Testament being literally fulfilled.

6. In view of such factors, it is both reasonable and consistent with the rest of biblical prophecy to hold that this passage refers to a yet-future invasion into Israel that will take place when Israel is in a state of security, likely after the rapture but before the tribulation period.

Israel Stands Alone

Israel will stand alone when attacked by the massive northern military coalition. Some nations—"Sheba, Dedan, the merchants of Tarshish" (apparently Saudi Arabia and some Western nations)—will diplomatically ask the invaders, "Have you come to seize spoil? Have you assembled your hosts to carry off plunder?" (Ezekiel 38:13). But their words are not followed by action. Israel stands utterly alone.

This means that the odds of Israel's survival, from a human perspective, will be nil. Israel will be vastly and overwhelmingly outnumbered. If this were merely a human battle, the outcome would be easy to predict. Israel will appear weak and alone in the face of this Goliath intruder, but God is strong! Ezekiel 38–39 reveals that the invading force will be annihilated by God before any damage falls upon Israel.

God Is Israel's Protector

God is all-powerful (Jeremiah 32:17). He has the power to do all that He desires and wills. Some 56 times Scripture declares that God is almighty (see Revelation 19:6, for example). God is abundant in strength (Psalm 147:5 NASB) and has incomparably great power (2 Chronicles 20:6; Ephesians 1:19-21). No one can hold back His hand (Daniel 4:35), reverse His actions (Isaiah 43:13), or thwart Him (Isaiah 14:27 NIV). Nothing is impossible with Him (Matthew 19:26; Mark 10:27; Luke 1:37), and nothing is too difficult for Him (Genesis 18:14; Jeremiah 32:17,27). The Almighty reigns (Revelation 19:6). Scripture reveals that this all-powerful God will utterly thwart the invasion of the northern military coalition.

Scripture also reveals that God is always watchful—"Behold, he who keeps Israel will neither slumber nor sleep" (Psalm 121:4)—and He will be Israel's defender. The invaders may think their success is all but guaranteed, but God sees all, and Israel's attackers stand no chance of success.

Recall that God had earlier promised His people that "no weapon that is fashioned against you shall succeed" (Isaiah 54:17). We often witness God fulfilling this promise in the Old Testament, playing the definitive role in battling against Israel's enemies (see, for example, Exodus 15:3 and Psalm 24:8). God is even sometimes described in military terms—the "LORD of hosts" (2 Samuel 6:2,18).

Ezekiel 38:18-19 mentions God's wrath and anger toward the northern military invaders. These words express the intensity of God's vengeance against those who attack His people.

God's multifaceted defeat of the northern military coalition, described for us in Ezekiel 38:17–39:8, will include a fourfold judgment.

1. An earthquake (Ezekiel 38:19-20). The devastating earthquake described by Ezekiel, in which "the mountains shall be thrown down, and the cliffs shall fall, and every wall shall tumble to the ground," will cause many troops to die. Transportation will be utterly disrupted, and apparently the armies of the multinational forces will be thrown into utter chaos.

2. Infighting (Ezekiel 38:21). God sovereignly induces the armies of the various nations in the invading force to turn on each other and kill each other. This may be at least partially due to the confusion and chaos that results following the massive earthquake. John F. Walvoord offered this explanation: "In the pandemonium, communication between the invading armies will break down and they will begin attacking each other. Every man's sword will be against his brother (Ezek. 38:21). Fear

and panic will sweep through the forces so each army will shoot indiscriminately at the others."[5] The armies of the various nations will also speak different languages—including Russian, Farsi, Arabic, and Turkic—making communication difficult and adding to the confusion. The Russians and Muslim nations may also turn on each other. Perhaps in the midst of the chaos, they will suspect they are being double-crossed and will respond by opening fire on each other. In any event, there will be countless casualties.

3. *Disease (Ezekiel 38:22)*. The earthquake and infighting will leave countless dead bodies in their wake. Transportation will be disrupted, hindering or preventing the transfer of wounded people, medicine, food and water, and other supplies. Meanwhile, birds and other predatory animals will feast on the unburied flesh. All this is a recipe for the outbreak of pandemic disease, which according to Ezekiel, will take many more lives.

4. *Torrential rain, hailstones, fire, and burning sulfur (Ezekiel 38:22)*. The fourth and final phase of God's execution of enemy forces will involve torrential rain (with heavy flooding), hailstones, fire, and burning sulfur pouring down on the invading troops. The powerful earthquake may trigger volcanoes in the region, thrusting into the atmosphere a hail of molten rock and burning sulfur (volcanic ash) that would fall on the invading troops, utterly destroying them.

What a turn of events all this will be. The invading troops will come with the intention of killing, but they themselves will be killed. They will believe their power is overwhelming, but they will be overwhelmed by the greater power of God. They will come to take over a new land (Israel) but instead will be buried in the land.

As if all this weren't enough, God also promises, "I will send fire on Magog and on those who dwell securely in the coastlands" (Ezekiel 39:6). The term Magog seems to refer to the southern part of the former Soviet Union—perhaps including the former southern Soviet republics of Kazakhstan, Kyrgyzstan, Uzbekistan, Turkmenistan, Tajikistan, and possibly even northern parts of modern Afghanistan. We are told in this prophetic verse that God will rain fire down upon this area of

the world and on Magog's allies "who dwell securely in the coastlands."
These sobering words have led Joel Rosenberg to make this comment:

> This suggests that targets throughout Russia and the for-
> mer Soviet Union, as well as Russia's allies, will be super-
> naturally struck on this day of judgment and partially or
> completely consumed. These could be limited to nuclear
> missile silos, military bases, radar installations, defense
> ministries, intelligence headquarters, and other govern-
> ment buildings of various kinds. But such targets could
> very well also include religious centers, such as mosques,
> madrassas, Islamic schools and universities, and other facil-
> ities that preach hatred against Jews and Christians and
> call for the destruction of Israel. Either way, we will have
> to expect extensive collateral damage, and many civilians
> will be at severe risk.[6]

This judgment will serve to nullify any possible reprisal or future
attempts at invasion. No further attack against Israel by these evil forces
will be possible!

The Burial of Enemy Bodies

Normally, when many are slain in a major battle and the battle is
over, the invaders bury their own dead. In the present case, however,
all the invaders will be dead, so the task of burial must fall to the house
of Israel.

Scripture reveals that the burial of these bodies will begin immediately after God destroys the northern military alliance. The number of
slain invaders will be so vast, so innumerable, that nothing but a deep
valley—the Valley of Hamon-gog—will suffice for their corpses (Ezekiel 39:11). And it will take a full seven months to accomplish the task
of burial in this valley. Keep in mind that the invaders come not from
a single nation, but rather from a coalition of nations, including Russia,
Iran, Turkey, Libya, and a number of other Muslim nations.

Following the seven-month period, a secondary burial crew will tra-
verse the land and search for any bones that were missed. This is all part

of the concerted effort to cleanse the land perfectly from all uncleanness arising from the bones of the dead (see Numbers 19:11-22; Deuteronomy 21:1-9). Markers will be placed wherever bones are found, and grave diggers will take the bones to the burial site.

The Gathering and Burning of Enemy Weapons

Following God's destruction of the northern military coalition, the Israelites will gather and burn enemy weapons for a period of seven years. If seven years is required to burn them all, that means a formidable arsenal will be collected.

Those interested in the precise chronology of biblical prophecy will note a problem here. If the seven years of burning weapons is parallel to the seven-year tribulation period, how can Israel take flight from Jerusalem in the middle of the tribulation? In Matthew 24, Jesus urges the Jews living in Jerusalem to take flight when the antichrist sets up his headquarters there in the middle of the tribulation. So the problem is this: How will the Jews be able to continue the task of burning weapons if they have to take flight from Jerusalem in the middle of the tribulation?

The problem can be avoided by not making the seven years of burning weapons parallel to the seven-year tribulation period. If the Ezekiel invasion takes place at least three and a half years prior to the beginning of the tribulation period (as I suggested earlier), the burning of weapons will be completed by the midpoint of the tribulation period.

Keep in mind that the tribulation does not begin directly after the rapture. Nothing in Scripture negates the possibility of a number of years passing between the rapture and the tribulation. The signal for the beginning of the tribulation is not the rapture, but rather the antichrist signing a covenant with Israel (Daniel 9:26-27).

The Conversion of Multitudes

In Ezekiel 38–39, God gives a mighty testimony of His power and glory in the midst of His destruction of the northern military coalition against Israel.

- "I will show my greatness and my holiness and make myself known in the eyes of many nations. Then they will know that I am the LORD" (Ezekiel 38:23).

- "My holy name I will make known in the midst of my people Israel, and I will not let my holy name be profaned anymore. And the nations shall know that I am the LORD, the Holy One in Israel" (Ezekiel 39:7).

- "I will set my glory among the nations, and all the nations shall see my judgment that I have executed, and my hand that I have laid on them. The house of Israel shall know that I am the LORD their God, from that day forward" (Ezekiel 39:21-22).

Clearly, God's destruction of the northern invaders will be a powerful testimony that no one can ignore. Indeed, the whole world will witness God's destruction of the invaders and recognize His greatness, holiness, and glory (38:23; 39:13,21). Moreover, Israel will be utterly awed at God's intervention on its behalf. God's stunning defeat of Gog and his military machine will force Israel to acknowledge His unfathomable power and justice (see Ezekiel 39:28-29).

A Shift in the Balance of Power

When God destroys the massive northern military coalition, the balance of political and religious power in the world will shift. This will make things much easier for the antichrist.

More specifically, the destruction of the northern invaders will pave the way for the antichrist to rise to power. With both Russia and a number of oil-wealthy Muslim nations out of the way, far fewer nations will have the political clout to challenge his authority when he comes into power early in the tribulation period. Arnold Fruchtenbaum makes this note: "The eastern balance of power will collapse with the fall of Russian forces and her Muslim allies in Israel and the destruction of Russia itself. With the eastern power destroyed, this will open the way for a one world government."[7]

As we have seen, this will also enable the antichrist to sign a peace pact with Israel (Daniel 9:27), guaranteeing that Israel will be protected. Muslim forces will no longer be a threat. As well, this likely explains why Israel is able to build its temple early in the tribulation period. After all, if the Muslims were still in power in the early part of the tribulation period and in control of the temple mount in Jerusalem, Israel would not be able to build its temple there. But if all the Muslim armies are largely destroyed by God prior to the beginning of the tribulation, this major obstacle to Israel's rebuilding of the temple is removed.

The Beginning of the Tribulation:
The Emergence of the Antichrist

IN THIS CHAPTER

The Antichrist Signs a Covenant

Scripture reveals that the single event that starts the tribulation period is the antichrist's signing of a covenant with Israel. This relates directly to Daniel's prophecy of seventy weeks.

In Daniel 9 God provided a prophetic timetable for the nation of Israel. The prophetic clock began ticking when the command went out to restore and rebuild Jerusalem following its destruction by Babylon (Daniel 9:25). According to this verse, Israel's timetable was divided into 70 groups of 7 years—a total of 490 years.

The first 69 groups of 7 years—or 483 years—counted the years "from the going out of the word to restore and rebuild Jerusalem to the coming of an anointed one, a prince" (Daniel 9:25). The Anointed One, or Messiah, is Jesus Christ. The day Jesus rode into Jerusalem to proclaim Himself Israel's Messiah was 483 years to the day after the command to restore and rebuild Jerusalem had been given.

At that point God's prophetic clock stopped. Daniel describes a gap between these 483 years and the final 7 years of Israel's prophetic time-table. Several events were to take place during this gap, according to Daniel 9:26: The Messiah would be killed, the city of Jerusalem and its temple would be destroyed (which occurred in AD 70), and the Jews would encounter difficulty and hardship from that time on.

The final "week" of seven years will begin for Israel when the anti-christ confirms a seven-year covenant (Daniel 9:27). The signing of this peace pact will signal the beginning of the tribulation period. It will begin the seven-year countdown to the second coming of Christ, which follows the tribulation period.

This seven-year time frame for the tribulation is reflected in other ancient Jewish literature, as Renald Showers shows in his helpful book *Maranatha: Our Lord Come!*

> The Babylonian Talmud states, "Our Rabbis taught: In the seven-year cycle at the end of which the son of David will come…at the conclusion of the septennate the son of David will come."

> Raphael Patai, writing on the Messianic texts, said, "The idea became entrenched that the coming of the Messiah will be preceded by greatly increased suffering…This will last seven years. And then, unexpectedly, the Messiah will come."[1]

The Day of the Lord

The antichrist's signing of the covenant with Israel constitutes not only the beginning of the tribulation period but also the beginning of the day of the Lord. The term *day of the Lord* is used in several senses in Scripture. The Old Testament prophets sometimes used it to describe an event to be fulfilled in the near future. At other times, they referred to an event in the distant eschatological future (the future tribulation period). The immediate context of the term generally indicates which sense is intended.

In both cases, the day of the Lord is characterized by God super-naturally intervening in order to bring judgment against sin in the world. The day of the Lord is a time in which God actively controls and dominates history in a direct way instead of working through secondary causes.

Among the New Testament writers, the term is generally used of the judgment that will climax in the end-time seven-year tribulation period (see 2 Thessalonians 2:2; Revelation 16–18) as well as the judgment that will usher in the new earth after the millennial kingdom (2 Peter 3:10-13; Revelation 20:7–21:1; see also Isaiah 65:17-19; 66:22; Revelation 21:1). This theme of judgment against sin runs like a thread through the many references to the day of the Lord.

A number of scriptural passages indicate that this aspect of the day of the Lord has not yet taken place but awaits the end times. For example, Isaiah 34:1-8 describes a day of the Lord in which God will judge all nations of the earth: "The LORD is enraged against all the nations… he has devoted them to destruction, has given them over for slaughter" (verse 2). None of the past days of the Lord ever involved divine judgment of *all* the nations. This indicates that the day of the Lord of Isaiah 34 must be yet future—that is, the tribulation period.

Similarly, Joel 3:1-16 and Zechariah 14:1-3,12-15 speak of a day of the Lord that will involve God's judgment of the armies of all the nations when they gather to wage war against Israel. We are told that the Jewish Messiah will come to war against these nations. This seems to coincide with Revelation 16:12-16, where we find that the armies will not begin to gather until the sixth bowl is poured out during the seventieth week of Daniel 9. Revelation 19:11-21 reveals that Christ will wage war against these armies when He comes from heaven to earth as King of kings and Lord of lords. Such facts force the conclusion that the day of the Lord spoken of by Joel 3 and Zechariah 14 is yet future.

Likewise, the apostle Paul in 1 Thessalonians 5:1-11 reveals that this eschatological day of the Lord is yet future. Paul warned that this day would bring sudden, inescapable destruction upon the unsaved of the world. The context of 1 Thessalonians 5 clearly points to the end-times tribulation period.

Because the antichrist's signing of the covenant with Israel begins the tribulation period, we can also say that this signing of the covenant begins the eschatological day of the Lord. Thankfully, Christians will escape this day because of the rapture.[2]

The Rise of the Antichrist

The apostle Paul warned of a "man of lawlessness," which is the antichrist (2 Thessalonians 2:3,8-9). Though sin and lawlessness are already at work in our own day (verse 7), Paul says a day is coming in which a specific individual will come into power in the future tribulation period who will be the embodiment of sin and lawlessness (compare with 1 John 2:18; Revelation 11:7; 13:1-10).

This lawless one will ultimately lead the entire world into rebellion against God (2 Thessalonians 2:10) as the son of destruction (verse 3). He is presently being restrained by the Holy Spirit, but after the rapture (when Christians indwelt by the Holy Spirit will be removed from the earth), he will be made manifest (verse 6) and will deceive multitudes (Revelation 19:20).

Scripture reveals that the antichrist will be a genius in intellect (Daniel 8:23), commerce (Daniel 11:43; Revelation 13:16-17), war (Revelation 6:2; 13:2), speech (Daniel 11:36), and politics (Revelation 17:11-12).

This individual will perform counterfeit signs and wonders and deceive many people during the future tribulation period (2 Thessalonians 2:9-10). In the book of Revelation, the apostle John describes this anti-God individual as a beast (Revelation 13:1-10).

This Satan-inspired individual will rise to prominence in the tribulation period, initially making a peace treaty with Israel (Daniel 9:27). In his desire to dominate the world, he will double-cross and then seek to destroy the Jews, persecute believers, and set up his own kingdom (Revelation 13). He will speak arrogant and boastful words, glorifying himself (2 Thessalonians 2:4). His assistant, the false prophet, will seek to make the world worship the antichrist (Revelation 13:11-12). The false prophet will control the global economy by forcing people around the world to receive the mark of the antichrist in order to buy or sell (Revelation 13:16-17). However, to receive this mark ensures one of being the recipient of God's wrath. The antichrist will eventually rule the whole world (Revelation 13:7) from his headquarters in Rome (Revelation 17:8-9). This beast will be defeated and bound by Jesus at His second coming (Revelation 19:11-16).

This is the big picture. Now let's consider some details about this evil person.

The Antichrist Will Not Be a Jew

Some interpreters have tried to argue that the antichrist will be a Jew. For example, an early tradition held that the antichrist would come from the tribe of Dan (one of the 12 tribes of Israel). Some relate this to the fact that the tribe of Dan fell into deep apostasy and idolatry, setting up a graven image (Judges 18:30). The Testament of Dan (5:6) names Satan as the prince of the tribe. Irenaeus, writing in the latter part of the second century, noted that the omission of Dan from the list of tribes in Revelation 7 was due to a tradition that the antichrist was to come from that tribe (*Adv. Haer.* v.30.2.).

However, Revelation 13:1 and 17:15 picture the antichrist as rising up out of the *sea*—a scriptural metaphor for the Gentile nations. Antiochus Epiphanes, himself a Gentile, typifies the future antichrist in Daniel 11. The antichrist is therefore not likely to be a Jew. Besides, he will persecute the Jews in the tribulation period (Jeremiah 30:7; Matthew 24:15-21; Revelation 12:6,13-14).

The Antichrist Will Not Be a Muslim

More recently, for understandable reasons, many have claimed that the antichrist will be a Muslim. However, this view has significant theological problems. For one thing, Daniel 11:36 tells us the antichrist "shall exalt himself and magnify himself above every god." We also read in 2 Thessalonians 2:4 that the antichrist ultimately "opposes and exalts himself against every so-called god or object of worship, so that he takes his seat in the temple of God, proclaiming himself to be God."

To say the very least, a Muslim antichrist who claimed to be God would be trashing the Muslim creed, "There is one God named Allah, and Muhammad is his prophet." No true Muslim would make any claim that he was God. Just as it is anathema to Muslims to call Jesus

"God incarnate" or the "Son of God," so it would be anathema to Muslims for any human to claim he was God. (Keep in mind that Muslims are radical monotheists.) A Muslim antichrist would thus be viewed as an infidel among Quran-believing Muslims.

Muslim teaching avows, "God can have no partners." Muslims generally quote this as an argument against the Christian doctrine of the Trinity, but it is certainly applicable to human leaders on earth who claim to be God. It is impossible to fathom a Muslim exalting himself to deity in this way.

Still further, Muslim teaching asserts that Allah is so radically unlike any earthly reality—so utterly transcendent and beyond anything in the finite realm—that he can scarcely be described using earthly terms. How, then, could a human, Muslim antichrist claim to be God? Again, it is impossible to fathom a Muslim describing himself in this way.

Also, why would a Muslim antichrist make a covenant with Israel, guaranteeing its protection (Daniel 9:24-27)? Many radical Muslims today want to push Israel into the sea or blow Israel off the map. A Muslim leader would not be likely to sign a covenant to protect Israel.

Still further, the Israelites—fully aware of Muslim animosity and hatred toward them—would never place their hopes of survival and security in the hands of a Muslim. Such a view makes no sense.

The Antichrist Will Not Be Gog

Contrary to the assumptions of some today, Gog (the leader of the invasion of Israel described in Ezekiel 38) is not the antichrist. Bible interpreters will end up in prophetic chaos if they try to make this identification.

The antichrist heads up a revived Roman Empire (Daniel 2; 7), but Gog heads up an invasion force made up of Russia and a number of Muslim nations (Ezekiel 38:1-6). Moreover, Gog's invasion into Israel constitutes a direct challenge to the antichrist's covenant with Israel (Daniel 9:27). Further, Gog's moment in the limelight is short-lived because God will destroy the invading force (Ezekiel 39), whereas the antichrist is in power over much of the seven-year tribulation.

The Antichrist Rises in a Revived Rome

Daniel 7:3-8 refers to four beasts. These represent kingdoms that play an important role in biblical prophecy. Daniel begins in verse 3 by affirming, "Four great beasts came up out of the sea, different from one another." These four beasts reveal much about prophetic chronology.

The first, Daniel says, was "like a lion and had eagles' wings," but "its wings were plucked off" (verse 4). This imagery apparently represents Babylon, its lion-like quality indicating power and strength. It is interesting to observe that winged lions guarded the gates of Babylon's royal palaces (see Jeremiah 4:7). The wings indicate rapid mobility, and the plucking of the wings indicates a removal of mobility (perhaps a reference to Nebuchadnezzar's insanity or to Babylon's deterioration following his death).

Daniel continued in verse 5. "And behold, another beast, a second one, like a bear. It was raised up on one side. It had three ribs in its mouth between its teeth; and it was told, 'Arise, devour much flesh.'" This is the Medo-Persia kingdom, and the ribs are vanquished nations—perhaps Lydia, Babylon, and Egypt. Medo-Persia was well-known for its strength and fierceness in battle (see Isaiah 13:17-18).

Daniel describes a third beast in verse 6. "And behold, another like a leopard, with four wings of a bird on its back. And the beast had four heads, and dominion was given to it." The leopard was known for its swiftness, cunning, and agility. This imagery represents Greece under Alexander the Great. The four heads depict the four generals who divided the kingdom following Alexander's death, ruling Macedonia, Asia Minor, Syria, and Egypt.

Finally, in verse 7, Daniel mentions the fourth beast—a mongrel that was more terrifying and powerful than the three preceding beasts.

> Behold, a fourth beast, terrifying and dreadful and exceedingly strong. It had great iron teeth; it devoured and broke in pieces and stamped what was left with its feet. It was different from all the beasts that were before it, and it had ten horns. I considered the horns, and behold, there came up among them another horn, a little one, before which three

of the first horns were plucked up by the roots. And behold,
in this horn were eyes like the eyes of a man, and a mouth
speaking great things.

This wild imagery refers to the Roman Empire. Rome already
existed in ancient days, but it fell apart in the fifth century AD. It will
be revived, however, in the end times, apparently comprised of ten
nations ruled by ten kings (ten horns). I noted previously in the book
that animals used their horns as weapons (see Genesis 22:3; Psalm
69:31). For this reason, the horn eventually came to be seen as a symbol of power and might. As an extension of this symbol, horns in biblical times were sometimes used as emblems of dominion, representing
kingdoms and kings, as is the case in the books of Daniel (chapters 7–8)
and Revelation (12:13; 13:1,11; 17:3-16).

In Daniel 7, an eleventh horn—a little horn (the antichrist)—starts
out apparently in an insignificant way but grows powerful enough to
uproot three of the existing horns (kings). He eventually comes into
absolute power and dominance over this revived Roman Empire, probably halfway through the tribulation period.

Related to this, Daniel 2 records a prophetic dream that Nebuchadnezzar had. In this dream, this end-times Roman Empire was pictured
as a mixture of iron and clay (see verses 41-43). Daniel, the great interpreter of dreams, saw this as meaning that just as iron is strong, so this
latter-day Roman Empire would be strong. But just as iron and clay
do not naturally mix with each other, so this latter-day Roman Empire
would have some divisions. It would not be completely integrated.

Many modern biblical interpreters see the European Union (which
is characterized by both unity and some division) as a primary prospect
for the ultimate fulfillment of this prophecy.[3] The stage is now appearing to be set for the fulfillment of Daniel 2 and 7. Once the antichrist
emerges into power in a revived Rome, it is just a matter of time before
he comes into complete global domination.

8

The Beginning of the Tribulation: The Temple and Signs of the End

The Jewish Temple Is Rebuilt

The temple has long played a prominent role in Jewish history. In fact, Israel has had three different temples.

The First Temple

David wanted to build the first temple for God, though it was not to happen, for David was disqualified for being a warrior. His son Solomon eventually built the temple (1 Kings 6–7; 2 Chronicles 3–4).

Like the tabernacle, Solomon's temple had a Holy Place and a Most Holy Place. The Holy Place (the main outer room) contained the golden incense altar, the table of showbread, five pairs of lampstands, and utensils used for sacrifice. Double doors led to the Holy of Holies, in which was found the ark of the covenant. The ark rested between two wooden cherubim angels, each standing ten feet tall. God manifested Himself in the Holy of Holies in a cloud of glory (1 Kings 8:10-11).

This temple—the heart and center of worship for the kingdom of Judah—was eventually destroyed by Nebuchadnezzar and the Babylonians in 587 BC.

The Second Temple

Following the Babylonian exile, many Jews returned to Jerusalem and constructed a smaller, leaner version of Solomon's temple. King Cyrus of Persia had allowed them to return and rebuild the temple, and he sent along the temple vessels Nebuchadnezzar had looted.

The returned exiles started out well in 538 BC but soon ran out of steam. The prophets Haggai and Zechariah worked hard to encourage them, and the second temple was finally completed in 515 BC. However, it was not nearly as magnificent as Solomon's temple (see Ezra 3:12). It had little of its former glory and was a dim reflection of the original. This temple was without the ark of the covenant and had only one seven-branched lampstand. The ark and Solomon's ten lampstands were never recovered. This temple lasted about 500 years.

The Third Temple

Israel's third temple in Jerusalem was built by King Herod the Great. Herod believed this ambitious building program, which he began in 19 BC, would be a great way to earn favor with the Jews of his time (that is, his subjects) and impress the Roman authorities.

Completed in AD 64, it was much larger and more resplendent (with more gold) than Solomon's temple. It was an enormous, cream-colored structure that shone exceedingly bright during the day. It measured 490 yards (north to south) by 325 yards (east to west).

This magnificent temple was destroyed along with the rest of Jerusalem by Titus and his Roman warriors in AD 70—a mere six years after the project was completed. How ironic that those Herod sought to impress in Rome were the instigators of the temple's destruction.

The Tribulation Temple

Scripture reveals that yet another temple will be built during the tribulation period. In terms of prophetic chronology, there are a number of important factors.

First and foremost is the prerequisite that Israel be back in her homeland as a nation. This has been a reality since 1948. The Jews have been streaming back to the holy land from around the world ever since (see Ezekiel 36–37). Obviously the Jewish temple cannot be rebuilt unless a reborn nation of Israel is in the land.

Second, we know that the temple must be rebuilt at least by the middle of the seven-year tribulation because Jesus in the Olivet discourse warned of a catastrophic event that assumes the existence of the temple: "When you see the abomination of desolation spoken of by the prophet Daniel, standing in the holy place (let the reader understand), then let those who are in Judea flee to the mountains" (Matthew 24:15-16). This abomination of desolation is the desecration of the Jewish temple by the antichrist, who will set up an image of himself within the temple at the midpoint of the tribulation. The temple must be built by this time.

It is significant that Jesus says this because just previously (in verses 1-2), He positively affirmed that the great temple built by Herod (the Jewish temple of Jesus's day) would be utterly destroyed: "Truly, I say to you, there will not be left here one stone upon another that will not be thrown down." This prophecy was literally fulfilled in AD 70 when Titus and his Roman warriors overran Jerusalem and the Jewish temple.

The only possible conclusion is that the temple of Jesus's day would be destroyed and that the abomination of desolation would occur in a yet-future temple. This latter temple would be built at least by the middle of the tribulation period (see also Daniel 9:27; 12:11).

Jewish Sacrifices Reinstated

Scripture is clear that there will be animal sacrifices in the Jewish temple sometime during the first half of the tribulation, but then the antichrist will stop them. We read in Daniel 9:27 that the antichrist "shall make a strong covenant with many for one week, and for half of the week he shall put an end to sacrifice and offering." This "week" refers to the seven-year tribulation period that precedes the second coming of Christ. For half of the week—that is, the last three and a half years—sacrifices in the temple will cease. John F. Walvoord explains it this way:

> This expression ["for half of the week he shall put an end to sacrifice and offering"] refers to the entire Levitical system, which suggests that Israel will have restored that system in the first half of the 70th seven. After this ruler gains worldwide political power, he will assume power in the religious realm as well and will cause the world to worship him (2 Thes. 2:4; Rev. 13:8). To receive such worship, he will terminate all organized religions. Posing as the world's rightful king and god and as Israel's prince of peace, he will then turn against Israel and become her destroyer and defiler.[1]

Preparations in the Present Day

Even today we hear reports that various Jewish individuals and groups have been working behind the scenes to prepare various materials for the future temple, including priestly robes, temple tapestries, and worship utensils. These items are being prefabricated so that when the temple is finally rebuilt, everything will be ready for it.

I reiterate that the temple does not need to be rebuilt until the midpoint of the tribulation period. This makes the fact that many items are already being prefabricated all the more exciting to many prophecy enthusiasts. The day of the rapture may be drawing near.

The Signs of the Times

A "sign of the times" is an event of prophetic significance that points to the end times. We might say that the signs of the times in the pages of prophetic Scripture constitute God's "intel in advance" regarding what the world will look like as we enter the end times.

We are specifically instructed that certain signs will take place as the tribulation period unfolds. In Matthew 24:3, the disciples asked Jesus, "What will be the sign of your coming and of the close of the age?" In verses 4 and following, Jesus mentions a number of signs of the times that will predominate during the tribulation period (just prior to the second coming).

Jesus urged His followers to be thoughtful observers of the times. He gave the Sadducees and Pharisees, who rejected Him as the divine Messiah, this challenge: "When it is evening, you say, 'It will be fair weather, for the sky is red.' And in the morning, 'It will be stormy today, for the sky is red and threatening.' You know how to interpret the appearance of the sky, but you cannot interpret the signs of the times" (Matthew 16:1-3).

These Jewish leaders were supposedly expert interpreters of the Old Testament Scriptures. In such messianic passages as Isaiah 11 and 35, we are told that when the Messiah came, the lame would walk, the deaf would hear, and the blind would see. When Jesus came on the scene, this is precisely what happened. These Jewish leaders should have been able to read the signs of the times and recognize that Jesus indeed was the promised Messiah. But they could not.

The lesson we learn from this is that you and I are called by Jesus to be thoughtful observers of the times. We are to be aware of what biblical prophecy teaches and then to keep a close eye on unfolding events in the world so that we become aware of any possible correlation between world events and biblical prophecy.

We are never to set dates (Matthew 24:36)—we do not know the specific day or hour of Jesus's coming (Acts 1:7)—but we can know the general season of the Lord's return by virtue of the signs of the times. Jesus urged His disciples, "Now learn the parable from the fig tree: when its branch has already become tender and puts forth its leaves, you know that summer is near; so, you too, when you see all these things, recognize that He is near, right at the door" (Matthew 24:32-33 NASB).

Jesus indicates in this passage that God has revealed certain things through prophecy (particularly related to the future tribulation period) that ought to cause people who know the Bible to understand that a fulfillment of prophecy is taking place—or perhaps, in our present day, the stage is being set for a prophecy to eventually be fulfilled. Jesus is thus informing His followers to be accurate observers of the times so that when biblical prophecies are fulfilled, or the stage is being set, they will realize what is happening (see also Luke 21:25-28).

Let us now briefly survey the signs of the times that Jesus described. I have categorized them as earth and sky signs, moral signs, religious signs, and technological signs.

Earth and Sky Signs

Scripture reveals that in the future tribulation period, earthquakes, famine, pestilence, and signs in the heavens will increase in frequency and intensity (Matthew 24:3,7). In Luke 21:11 (NIV) we read, "There will be great earthquakes, famines and pestilences in various places, and fearful events and great signs from heaven." Such things are said to be the beginning of "birth pains" (Matthew 24:8). Just as birth pains increase in frequency and intensity, so these signs will become more and more catastrophic.

These signs have particular relevance to the future seven-year tribulation period, but I believe that just as tremors (or foreshocks) often occur before major earthquakes, so preliminary manifestations of some of these signs may emerge prior to the tribulation period. Other people have said that prophecies cast their shadows before them. I think this is true. Prophecies that relate specifically to the tribulation are presently casting their shadows before them in our present day.

What are the "fearful events" mentioned in Luke 21:11 (NIV)? Scripture does not specify this for us, but the Greek phrase literally means "terror," "sights of terror," or "terrifying things." Terrorism has never been more prominent on a global basis than it is in our day. Terrorism will apparently get worse as we go into the future.

Signs in the heavens could include any number of different things, including strange weather patterns, falling stars, a darkening of the moon and other celestial bodies (specifically during the tribulation period), and large bodies striking the earth. For example, in the context of the future tribulation period, we find reference to "wormwood" in Revelation 8:10-12 (NASB):

> The third angel sounded, and a great star fell from heaven, burning like a torch, and it fell on a third of the rivers and

> on the springs of waters. The name of the star is called Wormwood; and a third of the waters became wormwood, and many men died from the waters, because they were made bitter.
>
> The fourth angel sounded, and a third of the sun and a third of the moon and a third of the stars were struck, so that a third of them would be darkened and the day would not shine for a third of it, and the night in the same way.

Many believe this "star" will in fact be a large meteor or asteroid striking the earth, causing a near-extinction-level "deep impact." It will look like a star because it will burst into flames, burning like a torch as it plummets through earth's atmosphere. It will turn a third of the waters bitter so that people who drink them will die. It may contaminate this large volume of water by the residue that results from the meteor disintegrating as it blasts through earth's atmosphere. Or the meteor may plummet into the headwaters from which some of the world's major rivers and underground water sources flow, thereby spreading the poisonous water to many people on earth.

Some scholars have speculated that this deep impact may be what causes a reduction in light from the sun and other celestial bodies. Following this impact, a catastrophic level of dust could be thrown into the atmosphere, blocking light (see Revelation 8:12).

Today's top scientists are saying that it is not a matter of *if* such a celestial body will strike earth, but *when*. The mathematical probabilities render this a certainty at some point in the future. And when it happens, it will likely involve a significant celestial body striking the earth with a minimum velocity of 130,000 miles per hour. The sad reality is that this event will, in fact, happen during the tribulation period, and the result will be truly catastrophic. Many will die!

Some have also speculated that the signs in the heavens may also include some UFO phenomena. Countless sightings of UFOs are reported around the world, and many today believe that "space brothers" are contacting us through psychics and mediums. I find it highly revealing that this "alien" contact is not through physical means, such as radios, but rather through the occult. Many of the "revelations" coming from the "space brothers" through physics deny essential doctrines of Christianity, including humanity's sin problem, the reality of hell, and the need to trust in Jesus Christ for salvation. Moreover, one must wonder why these "aliens" have come millions (billions?) of miles only to tell us the same kinds of things that New Agers have been telling us for decades.

Still further, one cannot help but notice that almost without exception, those claiming to have been abducted by aliens today have been involved in some form of the occult. Additionally, the typical abduction experience has notable similarities to occult Shamanistic initiation ceremonies.

I see Satan's fingerprints all over current UFO phenomena. Please do not get me wrong. I am not saying that every time somebody sees an unidentified flying object in the sky, it is the devil. As I document in my book *Alien Obsession: What Lies Behind Abductions, Sightings, and the Attraction to the Paranormal*, many times people are just seeing natural phenomena, such as space junk (more than 7000 pieces of space junk are floating around the earth), the planet Venus, ball lightning (a form of lightning that takes an oval shape, sizzles, and can move around the sky at great speeds, instantly changing directions), a high-flying weather balloon, a jet, or something else.

Nonetheless, a great deal of occult and psychic phenomena accompany current UFO incidents. Such phenomena have given rise to many "doctrines of demons," which prophetic Scripture reveals will characterize the end times (see 1 Timothy 4:1-2 NASB; see also 2 Timothy 4:3-4).

Moral Signs

Scripture also speaks of moral signs that will emerge during the future tribulation period.

> But realize this, that in the last days difficult times will come. For men will be lovers of self, lovers of money, boastful, arrogant, revilers, disobedient to parents, ungrateful, unholy, unloving, irreconcilable, malicious gossips, without

self-control, brutal, haters of good, treacherous, reckless, conceited, lovers of pleasure rather than lovers of God, holding to a form of godliness, although they have denied its power. Avoid such men as these (2 Timothy 3:1-5 NASB).

Notice that in the last days, people will love self (we might call this humanism), money (we might call this materialism), and pleasure (we might call this hedonism). It is significant that humanism, materialism, and hedonism are three of the most prominent philosophies in our world today, and they complement each other. Jesus Himself gave this warning:

Because lawlessness is increased, most people's love will grow cold…For the coming of the Son of Man will be just like the days of Noah. For as in those days before the flood they were eating and drinking, marrying and giving in marriage, until the day that Noah entered the ark, and they did not understand until the flood came and took them all away; so will the coming of the Son of Man be (Matthew 24:12,37-39).

This passage specifically refers to the future tribulation period, but we see the attitude Jesus described in our own day. People are merrily going about their way, seemingly with no concern for the things of God.

Without a doubt, America is engulfed in a moral crisis. The moral fiber of this country is eroding before our very eyes, and if the trend continues, it is only a matter of time before the country capitulates.

Today there is widespread acceptance of homosexuality. Abortion—even the barbaric practice of partial-birth abortion—continues to be widely practiced, with some 50 million unborn babies having been murdered since the enactment of *Roe v. Wade* in 1973. Pornography is pervasive and freely available on the Internet, enslaving millions as sex addicts.

Drug abuse and alcoholism are pervasive as well among both teenagers and adults. Promiscuity, fornication, and adultery continue to escalate to ever new heights, bringing about the carnage of sexually transmitted diseases.

Meanwhile, the family unit is disintegrating before our eyes. The divorce rate is around 50 percent, and many today are living together outside of marriage. Out-of-wedlock births have escalated to new highs, with 40 percent of women not being married when they give birth. As well, gay couples are adopting children, raising them in a homosexual atmosphere.

People are far more interested in happiness than in holiness. They yearn more for pleasure than for praising God. Humanism, material-ism, and hedonism reign in the end times!

Religious Signs

Prophetic Scripture refers to many religious signs that will find ful-fillment in the tribulation period (Matthew 24:3).

False christs. Jesus Himself warned about the end times: "For false messiahs and false prophets will appear and perform great signs and wonders to deceive, if possible, even the elect" (Matthew 24:24 NIV; see also Mark 13:22). The apostle Paul also warned of a different Jesus (2 Corinthians 11:4).

The danger, of course, is that a counterfeit Jesus who preaches a counterfeit gospel yields a counterfeit salvation (see Galatians 1:8). There are no exceptions to this maxim.

Even in our own day, we witness an unprecedented rise in false christs and self-constituted messiahs affiliated with the kingdom of the cults and the occult. This will no doubt continue as we move fur-ther into the end times.

False prophets and teachers. Scripture contains many warnings against false prophets and false teachers for the simple reason that God's own people can be deceived. Ezekiel 34:1-7, for example, indicates that God's sheep can be abused and led astray by wicked shepherds.

Jesus warned His followers, "Watch out for false prophets. They come to you in sheep's clothing, but inwardly they are ferocious wolves" (Matthew 7:15-16 NIV). Why would Jesus warn His followers to watch out if they could not possibly be deceived?

The apostle Paul warned Christians about the possibility of deception (Acts 20:28-30; 2 Corinthians 11:2-3). The Bible exhorts believers to test those who claim to be prophets (see 1 John 4:1-3). How can believers recognize a false prophet? False prophets may...

- offer prophecies that do not come true (Deuteronomy 18:21-22)
- cause people to follow false gods or idols (Exodus 20:3-4; Deuteronomy 13:1-3)
- deny the deity of Jesus Christ (Colossians 2:8-9)
- deny the humanity of Jesus Christ (1 John 4:1-2)
- forbid marriage and advocate abstaining from certain foods (1 Timothy 4:3-4)
- promote immorality (Jude 4-7)
- encourage legalistic self-denial (Colossians 2:16-23)

A basic rule of thumb is that if a so-called prophet says anything that clearly contradicts any part of God's Word, his teachings should be rejected (1 Thessalonians 5:21).

False apostles. The apostle Paul warned of false apostles who are "deceitful workmen, disguising themselves as apostles of Christ" (2 Corinthians 11:13). The two key characteristics we see here are that these individuals deceive people doctrinally and that they pretend to be true apostles of Jesus Christ.

Christ commends those who take a stand against false apostles. For example, He commended the church of Ephesus: "I know your deeds, your hard work and your perseverance. I know that you cannot tolerate wicked people, that you have tested those who claim to be apostles but are not, and have found them false" (Revelation 2:2 NIV).

How can we test the claims of apostles? Like the ancient Bereans, all Christians should make a regular habit of testing all things against Scripture (Acts 17:11), for Scripture is our only infallible barometer of truth. No true apostle will ever say anything that contradicts the Word of God (see Galatians 1:8).

Increasing apostasy. Scripture prophesies a great end-times apostasy involving a massive defection from the truth (Matthew 24:10-12; 2 Thessalonians 2:3). First Timothy 4:1-2 warns, "The Spirit expressly says that in later times some will depart from the faith by devoting themselves to deceitful spirits and teachings of demons, through the insincerity of liars whose consciences are seared." Likewise, 2 Timothy 4:3-4 warns, "The time is coming when people will not endure sound teaching, but having itching ears they will accumulate for themselves teachers to suit their own passions, and will turn away from listening to the truth and wander off into myths." Can any doubt that we are witnessing such things in our own day? Consider the things that people deny when they fall away:

> God (2 Timothy 3:4-5)
>
> Christ (1 John 2:22)
>
> Christ's return (2 Peter 3:3-4)
>
> the faith (1 Timothy 4:1-2)
>
> sound doctrine (2 Timothy 4:3-4)
>
> morals (2 Timothy 3:1-8)
>
> authority (2 Timothy 3:4)

We are living in days of deception!

Technological Signs

Certain technological advances must occur to make possible the fulfillment of some of the things specifically prophesied of the tribulation period in Scripture. We might call these technological signs. Many prophecy scholars believe that the technology is now in place for these things to occur.

Global evangelism. Matthew 24:14 tells us that prior to the second coming of Christ, the gospel must be preached to every nation. With today's technology—satellites, the Internet, global media, translation technologies, publishing technologies, rapid transportation, and the like—this has never been more possible.

Economic control. We do not know specifically what form the mark of the beast will take, but we do know that the false prophet will use it to control who will be able to buy and sell, depending on whether they submit to worshipping the antichrist (Revelation 13:16-17). With today's satellites, the Internet, supercomputers, biometric identification procedures (hand scanners, retina scanners, facial recognition scanners, and the like), RFID chips, and smart card technology, it would be easy for every selling establishment and every buyer to have a separate account number that would enable such control by the false prophet. This technology exists today!

Nuclear detonations? Prophetic Scripture may refer to nuclear detonations in the end times. For example, Revelation 8:7 tells us that "a third of the earth was burned up, and a third of the trees were burned up, and all the green grass was burned up." Moreover, Revelation 16:2 tells us that people around the world will break out with loathsome and malignant sores. Could this be a result of radiation poisoning following the detonation of nuclear weapons?

Some believe Jesus may have been alluding to nuclear weaponry when He spoke of "men fainting from fear and the expectation of the things which are coming upon the world; for the powers of the heavens will be shaken" (Luke 21:26 NASB). Whether or not this is so, the technology clearly now exists for a third of the earth to be burned up and for mass casualties.

Significance of the Signs of the Times

We have given brief consideration to earth and sky signs, moral signs, religious signs, and technological signs that relate to the future tribulation period. Even now, however, these prophetic signs are casting their shadows before them. They are emerging in preliminary form in our own day. We can logically infer that the stage is being set for the tribulation!

The First Half of the Tribulation: The Lamb and His Witnesses

The Lamb and the Seven-Sealed Scroll

In Revelation 5, we witness an awe-inspiring, Christ-exalting scene that takes place in heaven early in the tribulation period: Jesus Christ, the Lamb of God, receives the seven-sealed scroll.

> Then I saw in the right hand of him who was seated on the throne a scroll written within and on the back, sealed with seven seals. And I saw a strong angel proclaiming with a loud voice, "Who is worthy to open the scroll and break its seals?" And no one in heaven or on earth or under the earth was able to open the scroll or to look into it, and I began to weep loudly because no one was found worthy to open the scroll or to look into it. And one of the elders said to me, "Weep no more; behold, the Lion of the tribe of Judah, the Root of David, has conquered, so that he can open the scroll and its seven seals."

And between the throne and the four living creatures and among the elders I saw a Lamb standing, as though it had been slain, with seven horns and with seven eyes, which are the seven spirits of God sent out into all the earth. And he went and took the scroll from the right hand of him who was seated on the throne. And when he had taken the scroll, the four living creatures and the twenty-four elders fell down before the Lamb, each holding a harp, and golden bowls full of incense, which are the prayers of the saints. And they sang a new song, saying,

> Worthy are you to take the scroll
>   and to open its seals,
> for you were slain, and by your blood you
>   ransomed people for God
>   from every tribe and language and people and
>   nation,
> and you have made them a kingdom and priests
>   to our God,
>   and they shall reign on the earth.

Then I looked, and I heard around the throne and the living creatures and the elders the voice of many angels, numbering myriads of myriads and thousands of thousands, saying with a loud voice, "Worthy is the Lamb who was slain, to receive power and wealth and wisdom and might and honor and glory and blessing!" And I heard every creature in heaven and on earth and under the earth and in the sea, and all that is in them, saying, "To him who sits on the throne and to the Lamb be blessing and honor and glory and might forever and ever!" And the four living creatures said, "Amen!" and the elders fell down and worshiped.

The references to Christ as a Lamb and Lion refer to Christ's first coming and second coming respectively.

The Lion and the Lamb surely refer to Christ, with the Lamb referring to His first coming and His death and the

Lion referring to His second coming and His sovereign judgment of the world. This is the only place in Revelation where Christ is called a Lion, whereas the word "Lamb" (*arnion*, "a small or young lamb") is found 27 times in Revelation and nowhere else in the New Testament.[1]

This Lamb who is a Lion is all-powerful. Earlier, I noted that animals use their horns as weapons and that horns eventually came to be seen as symbols of power and might. As an extension of this symbol, horns in biblical times were sometimes used as emblems of dominion, representing kingdoms and kings, as is the case in the books of Daniel and Revelation (see Daniel 7–8; Revelation 13:1,11; 17:3-16). The number seven in the Bible indicates completeness or perfection. Christ's seven horns therefore point to His complete dominion and omnipotence. The "seven spirits of God" apparently point to the Holy Spirit (see Revelation 1:4; 4:5).

Because this Lamb and Lion was found worthy, He "took the scroll from the right hand of him who was seated on the throne." This reminds us of Daniel 7:13-14:

> I saw in the night visions, and behold, with the clouds of heaven there came one like a son of man, and he came to the Ancient of Days and was presented before him. And to him was given dominion and glory and a kingdom, that all peoples, nations, and languages should serve him; his dominion is an everlasting dominion, which shall not pass away, and his kingdom one that shall not be destroyed.

How awesome it is to ponder such heavenly scenes involving the Father and the Son, the first and second persons of the Trinity!

After the Lamb who is a Lion takes the scroll from Him who sits on the throne, the 24 elders fall down and worship Him. This of course is as it should be, for Christ, as God, has always been worshipped (Hebrews 1:6). Even during His time on earth, Jesus accepted worship from…

Thomas (John 20:28)

the wise men (Matthew 2:11)

a leper (Matthew 8:2)

a ruler (Matthew 9:18)

a blind man (John 9:38)

a woman (Matthew 15:25)

Mary Magdalene (Matthew 28:9)

the disciples (Matthew 28:17)

If you've read the book of Acts lately, you might recall that the apostle Paul and Barnabas miraculously healed a man in Lystra by God's mighty power, and those who were in the crowd shouted, "The gods have come down to us in the likeness of men!" (Acts 14:11). But Paul and Barnabas would have none of it. "They tore their garments and rushed out into the crowd, crying out, 'Men, why are you doing these things? We also are men, of like nature with you'" (verses 14-15). As soon as they perceived what was happening, they immediately corrected the gross misconception that they were gods.

By contrast, Jesus never sought to correct His followers when they bowed down and worshipped Him. Rather, He considered such worship as perfectly appropriate. That He accepted worship and did not correct those who worshipped Him is yet another affirmation that He truly was God in the flesh.

When Christ is worshipped in this heavenly scene in Revelation 5, it is a clear recognition not only that He is worthy but also that He is indeed God. In fact, the elders are joined by the hosts of angels in heaven, who collectively render praise to the Lamb in a loud voice. Then every creature in heaven and on earth join in praise to God.

This wondrous scene in heaven sets the stage for all that follows, for now we will witness the actual opening of the seven seals. And as the seals are opened, one by one, we witness judgments falling on those on earth at the hand of our sovereign and majestic God. How awesome and sobering it will be!

The 144,000 Jewish Evangelists

In Revelation 7:4 (NIV), the apostle John writes, "Then I heard the number of those who were sealed: 144,000 from all the tribes of Israel." Who are these 144,000?

Some Christians have taken this as metaphorically referring to the church. However, the context indicates the verse is referring to 144,000 Jewish men—12,000 from each tribe—who live during the future tribulation period (see Revelation 14:4). The very fact that specific tribes are mentioned in this context, along with specific numbers for those tribes, removes all possibility that this is a figure of speech. Nowhere else in the Bible does a reference to 12 tribes of Israel mean anything but 12 tribes of Israel. Indeed, the word *tribe* is never used of anything but a literal ethnic group in Scripture.

The backdrop to a proper understanding of the 144,000 during the tribulation is that God had originally chosen the Jews to be His witnesses. He appointed them to share the good news of God with all other people around the world (see Isaiah 42:6; 43:10). The Jews were to be God's representatives to the Gentile peoples. Biblical history reveals that the Jews failed at this task, especially when they didn't recognize Jesus as the divine Messiah. During the future tribulation, these 144,000 Jews—who become believers in Jesus the divine Messiah sometime following the rapture—will finally fulfill this mandate from God and be His witnesses all around the world. Their work will yield a mighty harvest of souls (see Revelation 7:9-14).

These witnesses will be "sealed" (divinely protected) by God as they carry out their service for Him during the tribulation (Revelation 14:1-4; see also 2 Corinthians 1:22; Ephesians 1:13; 4:30).

Some have wondered why the Old Testament tribes of Dan and Ephraim are omitted from this list of Jewish tribes. The Old Testament has some 20 variant lists of tribes, so no two lists of the 12 tribes of Israel must be identical. Most scholars today agree that Dan's tribe was omitted because that tribe was guilty of idolatry on many occasions and, as a result, was largely obliterated (Leviticus 24:11; Judges 18:1,30; see also 1 Kings 12:28-29). To engage in unrepentant idolatry is to be cut off from God's blessing. The tribe of Ephraim was also involved in idolatry and paganized worship (Judges 17; Hosea 4:17). This is probably why both tribes were omitted from Revelation 7.

Others have wondered why the tribe of Levi was included in this list of Jewish tribes rather than maintaining its special status as a priestly tribe under the Mosaic law. Levi is probably included here because the priestly functions of the tribe of Levi ceased with the coming of Christ, the ultimate high priest. Indeed, the Levitical priesthood was fulfilled in the person of Christ (Hebrews 7–10). With no further need for the services of the tribe of Levi as priests, God had no further reason for keeping this tribe distinct and separate from the others. This is probably why they were properly included in the tribal listing in the book of Revelation.

As for the chronology of when these 144,000 Jewish evangelists emerge on the scene, I personally believe this event occurs in the early part of the tribulation period, sometime after the rapture. Some Bible expositors suggest that the 144,000 must engage in their work of evangelism early in the tribulation, for the believers who are martyred in the fifth seal judgment (Revelation 6:9-11) are among the fruit of their labors, and the seal judgments are definitely in the first half of the tribulation period.[2]

These Jews will probably become believers in Jesus in a way similar to that of the apostle Paul, himself a Jew, who had a Damascus-road encounter with the risen Christ (see Acts 9:1-9). Interestingly, in 1 Corinthians 15:8, the apostle Paul refers to himself in his conversion to Christ as "one untimely born." Some Bible expositors, such as J. Dwight Pentecost, believe Paul may have been alluding to his 144,000 Jewish tribulation brethren, who would be spiritually "born" in a way similar to him—only Paul was spiritually born far before them.

God's Two Prophetic Witnesses

During the tribulation period, God will raise up two mighty witnesses who will testify to the true God with astounding power. In fact, the power of these witnesses bring to mind Elijah (1 Kings 17; Malachi 4:5) and Moses (Exodus 7–11). In the Old Testament, two witnesses were required to confirm testimony (see Deuteronomy 17:6; 19:15; Matthew 18:16; John 8:17; Hebrews 10:28).

I will grant authority to my two witnesses, and they will prophesy for 1,260 days, clothed in sackcloth.

These are the two olive trees and the two lampstands that stand before the Lord of the earth. And if anyone would harm them, fire pours from their mouth and consumes their foes. If anyone would harm them, this is how he is doomed to be killed. They have the power to shut the sky, that no rain may fall during the days of their prophesying, and they have power over the waters to turn them into blood and to strike the earth with every kind of plague, as often as they desire (Revelation 11:3-6).

These witnesses will wear clothing made of goat or camel hair, garments that symbolically express mourning over the wretched condition and lack of repentance in the world. The reference to olive trees and lampstands is intended to symbolize the light of spiritual revival. Those who stand against these two witnesses will encounter a fiery response!

Many expositors believe the two witnesses will actually be Moses and Elijah. Here are three of the reasons for this view.

- The tribulation is a period in which God deals with the Jews—just as He did in the first 69 weeks (that is, weeks of years) of Daniel. Moses and Elijah are two of the most influential figures in Jewish history.

- Moses and Elijah appeared on the mount of transfiguration with Jesus. This shows their centrality.

- The miracles portrayed in Revelation 11 are very similar to those previously performed by Moses and Elijah in Old Testament times.

These reasons are valid, but one cannot be dogmatic. The two witnesses may be two entirely new prophets of God.

Scholars debate whether the ministry of the two witnesses belongs in the first half or the second half of the tribulation. Their ministry will last 1260 days, which measures out to precisely three and a half years.

Obviously, this is equivalent to half of the tribulation period. However, the context of Revelation 11 does not reveal whether this is the first or second half of the tribulation.

Most prophecy scholars conclude that the two witnesses do their miraculous work during the first three and a half years. The reason is that the antichrist's execution of them seems to fit best with other events that will transpire in the middle of the tribulation—such as the antichrist's exaltation of himself to godhood in defiance of the true God and His witnesses.

Moreover, the resurrection of the two witnesses—after being dead for three days—would make a much bigger impact on the world in the middle of the tribulation than at the end, when Armageddon is in full swing, just prior to the second coming of Christ.

In any event, the martyrdom of the two witnesses—apparently at the midpoint of the tribulation—is described in detail in Revelation 11:7-12:

> When they have finished their testimony, the beast that rises from the bottomless pit will make war on them and conquer them and kill them, and their dead bodies will lie in the street of the great city that symbolically is called Sodom and Egypt, where their Lord was crucified. For three and a half days some from the peoples and tribes and languages and nations will gaze at their dead bodies and refuse to let them be placed in a tomb, and those who dwell on the earth will rejoice over them and make merry and exchange presents, because these two prophets had been a torment to those who dwell on the earth. But after the three and a half days a breath of life from God entered them, and they stood up on their feet, and great fear fell on those who saw them. Then they heard a loud voice from heaven saying to them, "Come up here!" And they went up to heaven in a cloud, and their enemies watched them.

This resurrection will serve as a mighty testimony to the power of God during the tribulation. How awesome a day this will be. (I will address these two witnesses again in chapter 11, which deals with events at the midpoint of the tribulation.)

10

The First Half of the Tribulation: Judgments, Martyrdom, and Apostasy

The Seal Judgments Are Unleashed

The God of heaven—whose glory and majesty we witnessed in Revelation 6—is all-powerful and sovereign over all things in the universe, but He is also a God of judgment. In his modern classic *Knowing God*, J.I. Packer forcefully reminds us of this sobering, oft-forgotten truth.

> The reality of divine judgment, as a fact, is set forth on page after page of Bible history. God judged Adam and Eve, expelling them from the Garden and pronouncing curses on their future earthly life (Gen. 3). God judged the corrupt world of Noah's day, sending a flood to destroy mankind (Gen. 6–8). God judged Sodom and Gomorrah, engulfing them in a volcanic catastrophe (Gen. 18–19). God judged Israel's Egyptian taskmasters, just as

He foretold He would (see Gen. 15:14), unleashing against them the terrors of the ten plagues (Ex. 7–12). God judged those who worshipped the golden calf, using the Levites as His executioners (Ex. 32:26-35). God judged Nadab and Abihu for offering Him strange fire (Lev. 10:1ff.), as later He judged Korah, Dathan, and Abiram, who were swallowed up in an earth tremor. God judged Achan for sacrilegious thieving; he and his family were wiped out (Josh. 7). God judged Israel for unfaithfulness to Him after their entry into Canaan, causing them to fall under the dominion of other nations (Judg. 2:11ff., 3:5ff., 4:1ff.).[1]

Some people have tried to claim that the God of the Old Testament is characterized by judgment, whereas the God of the New Testament is all about love. God *is* a God of love, but He also continues to be a God of judgment in the New Testament. Judgment falls on the Jews for rejecting Jesus Christ (Matthew 21:43), on Ananias and Sapphira for lying to God (Acts 5), on Herod for his self-exalting pride (Acts 12:21-23), and on Christians in Corinth who were afflicted with serious illness and even death in response to their irreverence in connection with the Lord's Supper (1 Corinthians 11:29-32; see also 1 John 5:16). Christians will one day stand before the judgment seat of Christ (1 Corinthians 3:12-15; 2 Corinthians 5:10). Unbelievers will be judged at the great white throne (Revelation 20:11-15).

The Tribulation Period

It is no surprise to witness various judgments falling upon the world during the future tribulation period. Interestingly, the word *tribulation* comes to us from a Latin word meaning "to press" (as grapes). It refers to times of oppression, affliction, and distress. The Greek word *thlipsis* is translated variously as "tribulation," "affliction," "anguish," "persecution," "trouble," and "burden." This word has been used in relation to...

- those "hard pressed" by the calamities of war (Matthew 24:21)

- a woman giving birth to a child (John 16:21)

- the afflictions of Christ (Colossians 1:24)
- those "pressed" by poverty and lack (Philippians 4:14)
- great anxiety and burden of heart (2 Corinthians 2:4)
- a period in the end times that will have unparalleled tribulation (Revelation 7:14)

General tribulation is to be distinguished from the end-times tribulation period. All Christians may expect a certain amount of general tribulation in their lives. Jesus Himself said to the disciples, "In the world you will have tribulation" (John 16:33). Paul and Barnabas also warned that "through many tribulations we must enter the kingdom of God" (Acts 14:22). But the end-times tribulation period is distinct.

- Scripture refers to a definite period of time of tribulation at the end of the age (Matthew 24:29-35).
- It will be of such severity that no period in history past or future will equal it (verse 21).
- It will be shortened for the sake of the elect (verse 22), as no flesh could survive it.
- It is called the time of Jacob's trouble, for it is a judgment on Messiah-rejecting Israel (Jeremiah 30:7; Daniel 12:1-4).
- The nations will also be judged for their sin and rejection of Christ (Isaiah 26:21; Revelation 6:15-17).
- This tribulation period will last seven years (Daniel 9:24,27).
- This period will be so bad that people will want to hide and even die (Revelation 6:16).

The Unleashing of Judgments

The book of Revelation indicates that human suffering will steadily escalate during the tribulation period. The first set of judgments to be unleashed on earth are the seal judgments. Consider the horror of these judgments:

First seal judgment. The rider of the white horse—the antichrist—goes out to conquer and make war (Revelation 6:1-2).

Second seal judgment. Peace is taken from the earth, with people slaying each other on a massive level (verses 3-4).

Third seal judgment. Widespread famine emerges, probably as a result of war breaking out on a global scale, causing a disruption in transportation and distribution of food supplies (verses 5-6).

Fourth seal judgment. Massive casualties result from the widespread famine and pestilence, further aggravated by predatory wild beasts (verses 7-8).

Fifth seal judgment. Massive numbers of God's people are mercilessly martyred (verses 9-11).

Sixth seal judgment. A devastating earthquake is accompanied by severe cosmic disturbances. People everywhere try to hide (verses 12-17). Further cosmic disturbances will occur a little later in the tribulation period. A third of the sun, moon, and stars will be darkened at the fourth trumpet (8:12), the sun will be darkened by smoke from the abyss at the fifth trumpet (9:1-2), and the sun will scorch people with fire and fierce heat when the fourth bowl is poured out (16:8-9).

Seventh seal judgment. This final seal judgment results in the unleashing of the trumpet judgments, which are even more catastrophic.

Parallels to Jesus's Olivet Discourse

In Jesus's Olivet discourse, He speaks of things that will occur during the first half of the tribulation period, and more than a few Bible expositors have noticed the parallels that seem to exist between these events and the seal judgments.

Jesus's Olivet Discourse (Matthew 24)	The Seal Judgments (Revelation 6)
false christs (verses 4-5)	the antichrist (verses 1-2)
wars and rumors of war (verse 6)	men slay one another (verses 3-4)
famines (verse 7)	famine (verses 5-6)
earthquakes (verse 7)	a great earthquake (verses 12-14)

A comparison of Matthew 24 and Revelation 6 seems to indicate that these horrific events occur during the first half of the tribulation period. Woe to those who live on earth during this time, for things are about to get even worse.

Martyrdom Increases

Scripture reveals that even though the church will be raptured prior to the tribulation period (1 Thessalonians 1:10; 4:13-17; 5:9; Revelation 3:10), many people will become believers during the tribulation period. (These are the "sheep" of Matthew 25:31-46.) There will be many conversions (Revelation 7:9-10).

Though many believers in Jesus will still be alive at the time of the second coming, which occurs after the tribulation (see Matthew 25:31-46), many others will be martyred during the tribulation. We have already noted the martyrdom in connection with the fifth seal judgment in Revelation 6:9-11:

> When he opened the fifth seal, I saw under the altar the souls of those who had been slain for the word of God and for the witness they had borne. They cried out with a loud voice, "O Sovereign Lord, holy and true, how long before you will judge and avenge our blood on those who dwell on the earth?" Then they were each given a white robe and told to rest a little longer, until the number of their fellow servants and their brothers should be complete, who were to be killed as they themselves had been.

This passage indicates that not only are many already martyred, but more are yet to come, even in the early days of the tribulation period. Some of these martyred "fellow servants" are the "great multitude" mentioned in Revelation 7:9-17—"the ones coming out of the great tribulation" who "have washed their robes and made them white in the blood of the Lamb" (verse 14). Some of this great multitude may die natural deaths, but most will likely die as martyrs, as Bible expositor Thomas Constable explains.

This group appears to be the same as the one referred to earlier in 6:9-11 (cf. v. 14). These believers died either natural or
violent deaths during the first half of the Tribulation. They
have joined the angels in the heavenly throne-room that
John saw previously (chs. 4–5; cf. v. 11). Now they hold
palm branches symbolizing their victory and joy (cf. John
12:13). They are worshipping and serving God in heaven…
They will no longer experience the privations and discom-
forts of their earthly existence (cf. Isa. 49:10 [LXX]; John
4:14; 6:35; 7:37). The Lamb, now seen standing before the
middle of the throne, will provide for them as a good shep-
herd takes care of his sheep (cf. Ps. 23:1-4; Isa. 40:11; Ezek.
34:23; John 10:11,14; Heb. 13:20; 1 Pet. 2:25; 5:2-4).[2]

The book of Revelation indicates that such martyrdom in the tribulation period will be nothing new. In Revelation 2 Christ speaks to
the church in Pergamum about one of His faithful martyrs: "I know
where you dwell, where Satan's throne is. Yet you hold fast my name,
and you did not deny my faith even in the days of Antipas my faithful witness, who was killed among you, where Satan dwells" (verse 13).

Christ urges His people to stand strong and not fear martyrdom.
When He comforted the church in Smyrna, He included this exhor-
tation: "Do not fear what you are about to suffer. Behold, the devil is
about to throw some of you into prison, that you may be tested, and
for ten days you will have tribulation. Be faithful unto death, and I will
give you the crown of life" (Revelation 2:10).

God's people will be persecuted during the tribulation period, and
some will be killed. But death will simply be the gateway to eternal life
with Jesus Christ, the divine Messiah.

The Trumpet Judgments Are Unleashed

Revelation 8 indicates that the seal judgments, as bad as they are,
are followed by even worse judgments—the trumpet judgments.

First trumpet judgment. Hail and fire fall upon the earth. We are told
that "a third of the earth was burned up, and a third of the trees were
burned up, and all green grass was burned up" (verse 7). Some modern

prophecy scholars suggest the possibility of nuclear detonations in this judgment. After all, what else could burn up a third of the earth?

Second trumpet judgment. A fiery mountain plummets into the sea, which turns bloody, resulting in a third of the sea creatures dying (verse 8). This, of course, cuts into the food supply as well as fouling the waters of the sea.

Third trumpet judgment. A star falls from heaven (verses 10-11). As noted previously, many believe this "star" will be a large meteor or an asteroid striking the earth and causing a near-extinction-level "deep impact." It looks like a star because it bursts into flames as it plummets through earth's atmosphere. It results in turning a third of the waters bitter so that people who drink them die.

Fourth trumpet judgment. Severe cosmic disturbances emerge. We are told that "a third of the sun was struck, and a third of the moon, and a third of the stars, so that a third of their light might be darkened, and a third of the day might be kept from shining, and likewise a third of the night" (verses 12-13). The diminishing of light may be due to the massive dust kicked up into the atmosphere when the large meteor or asteroid associated with the third trumpet judgment strikes the earth. With the diminishing of light, the growth of plant life will be hindered, thereby furthering reducing the food supply.

Fifth trumpet judgment. Hideous demons are released from the bottomless pit, and they engage in relentless torment of human beings for five months (Revelation 9:1-12). During this time, people will seek death but will not be able to escape their pain. They will long for death rather than repent before a holy God.

Sixth trumpet judgment. Angels that are bound at the Euphrates are released, and they kill a third of humankind by plagues (verses 13-21). Amazingly, "the rest of mankind, who were not killed by these plagues, did not repent of the works of their hands nor give up worshiping demons and idols of gold and silver and bronze and stone and wood, which cannot see or hear or walk, nor did they repent of their murders or their sorceries or their sexual immorality or their thefts" (verses 20-21). The hearts of human beings will be calloused and hardened against God.

Seventh trumpet judgment. This final trumpet judgment results in the unleashing of the bowl judgments, which are even worse than the trumpet judgments (see Revelation 16). How awful it will be for those dwelling on the earth. Those who have experienced the trumpet judgments will think that things are as bad as they can possibly be. But God's judgments will continue to escalate in the bowl judgments.

Religious Babylon Dominates the World

In Revelation 17 we find prophecies of religious Babylon. Verses 1-7 describe it, and verses 8-18 interpret John's vision, which includes much symbolic language.

The passage indicates that religious Babylon is a great prostitute whose religious unfaithfulness influences the people of many nations. Revelation 17:1 tells us that this prostitute is "seated on many waters," which symbolizes various peoples, multitudes, nations, and languages. Scripture reveals that the kings of the earth commit adultery with this harlot and become a part of the religious system she symbolizes (see Revelation 14:8). This false religious system apparently emerges during the first half of the tribulation period.

This great prostitute—a truly blasphemous religion—sits on (and thus controls) a scarlet beast, who is the antichrist. Prostitution is often a graphic metaphor in Scripture that symbolizes unfaithfulness to God, idolatry, and religious apostasy (see Jeremiah 3:6-9; Ezekiel 20:30; Hosea 4:15; 5:3; 6:10; 9:1).

We also read of "seven mountains on which the woman is seated" (Revelation 17:9). Apparently, the seven mountains symbolize the seven kingdoms and their kings that are mentioned in verse 10. Mountains often symbolize kingdoms in Scripture (see, for example, Psalm 30:7; Jeremiah 51:25; Daniel 2:44-45).

These seven kingdoms refer to the seven great world empires—Egypt, Assyria, Babylon, Medo-Persia, Greece, Rome, and that of the antichrist. The biblical text tells us that five of these kingdoms have fallen, one still exists, and one is yet to come (Revelation 17:10). This means that at the time of John's writing, the Egyptian, Assyrian, Babylonian, Medo-Persian, and Greek empires had fallen. Rome, however, still existed during John's day, and the antichrist's kingdom was yet to come in the end times. This passage tells us that false paganized religion has affected (or will affect) all these empires.

Revelation 17 indicates that this apostate religious system will...

- be worldwide (verse 15)
- be utterly unfaithful to the truth and therefore a "harlot" (verses 1,5,15-16)
- exercise powerful political clout among the nations (verses 12-13)
- seem outwardly glorious while being inwardly corrupt (implied in verse 4)
- persecute believers during the tribulation period (verse 6)

11

The Midpoint of the Tribulation

The Little Scroll Is Opened

In Revelation 10, we read of an angel with a mysterious little scroll. The biblical description is intriguing.

> Then I saw another mighty angel coming down from heaven, wrapped in a cloud, with a rainbow over his head, and his face was like the sun, and his legs like pillars of fire. He had a little scroll open in his hand. And he set his right foot on the sea, and his left foot on the land, and called out with a loud voice, like a lion roaring. When he called out, the seven thunders sounded. And when the seven thunders had sounded, I was about to write, but I heard a voice from heaven saying, "Seal up what the seven thunders have said, and do not write it down." And the angel whom I saw standing on the sea and on the land raised his right hand to heaven and swore by him who lives forever and ever, who created heaven and what is in it, the earth and what is in it, and the sea and what is in it, that there would be no more delay, but that in the days of the trumpet call to be sounded by the seventh angel, the mystery of God would be fulfilled, just as he announced to his servants the prophets.
>
> Then the voice that I had heard from heaven spoke to me again, saying, "Go, take the scroll that is open in the hand of the angel who is standing on the sea and on the land." So I went to the angel and told him to give me the little scroll. And he said to me, "Take and eat it; it will make your stomach bitter, but in your mouth it will be sweet as honey." And I took the little scroll from the hand of the angel and ate it. It was sweet as honey in my mouth, but when I had eaten it my stomach was made bitter. And I was told, "You must again prophesy about many peoples and nations and languages and kings."

The Apocalypse provides revelation to God's people about the future. As we see in this passage, however, John was forbidden to record what the seven thunders spoke. Nevertheless, what was recorded was to have no further delay. An announcement was made that the seventh trumpet would bring about the accomplishment of the mystery of God.

What is this mystery of God? Prophecy expositors have various opinions. John F. Walvoord offers this explanation: "[God's] mystery had been previously announced to God's prophets. The reference, therefore, is not to hidden truth but to the fulfillment of *many* Old Testament passages which refer to the glorious return of the Son of God and the establishment of His kingdom of righteousness and peace on the earth."[1] William MacDonald and Arthur Farstad suggest that "the mystery of God has to do with God's plan to punish all evildoers and to usher in the kingdom of His Son."[2] Arnold Fruchtenbaum suggests that "the content of the Little Book is prophecy, especially the prophecy of the middle and the second half of the Tribulation."[3] It is unwise to be dogmatic about this mystery.

John obeyed the angel's instruction to eat the scroll, and though it was sweet (like honey) in his mouth, it quickly soured in his stomach. The symbol seems to relate to Scripture. God's Word was sweet to John, as it is sweet to believers around the world, throughout all ages. After all, the Word of God abounds with the glorious promises of God. The Word of God speaks of victory in the end for God's people. However, the Word of God is bitter to unbelievers because it includes warnings of woe and judgment. Scripture promises doom, not victory, for those who have rejected God. This passage depicts both sweetness and bitterness in the Word of God.

Fruchtenbaum suggests that this approaching tribulation bitterness for unbelievers ought to give us a burden for the lost so that some may be reached for Christ and escape the coming tribulation through the rapture of the church.[4] That, of course, requires that people trust in the divine Messiah now, for salvation is found only in Him (John 14:6; Acts 4:12).

The Antichrist Is Wounded and Is Seemingly Resurrected

In Revelation 13:1-3, we read of the apparent death and resurrection of the antichrist.

> I saw a beast rising out of the sea, with ten horns and seven
> heads, with ten diadems on its horns and blasphemous
> names on its heads. And the beast that I saw was like a leop-
> ard; its feet were like a bear's, and its mouth was like a lion's
> mouth. And to it the dragon gave his power and his throne
> and great authority. One of its heads seemed to have a mor-
> tal wound, but its mortal wound was healed, and the whole
> earth marveled as they followed the beast.

This has been the topic of much debate and speculation. Some have suggested this may refer to the revival of the Roman Empire, and that people will be amazed when it happens. However, this view has problems, as prophecy scholar Arnold Fruchtenbaum notes: "A revived Roman Empire would not cause man to worship it as God any more than the revival of Poland or Israel did. This kind of thinking is purely imaginary. It is the resurrection of the man Antichrist which creates this worship."[5]

Many other Bible-believing prophecy lovers believe this refers to the antichrist suffering a mortal head wound and then somehow being healed by Satan. In keeping with this, Revelation 13:12 clarifies things a bit in its reference to "the first beast, whose fatal wound had been healed." John F. Walvoord explains it this way:

> The final world ruler receives a wound which normally
> would be fatal but is miraculously healed by Satan. While
> the resurrection of a dead person seems to be beyond
> Satan's power, the healing of a wound would be possible
> for Satan, and this may be the explanation. The important
> point is that the final world ruler comes into power obvi-
> ously supported by a supernatural and miraculous deliver-
> ance by Satan himself.[6]

This supernatural event would seem to be a contributing factor to people worshipping the antichrist, for many will believe that this involves a godlike recovery. Many will be awestruck.

Satan's Power

Walvoord touches upon an important issue: Does Satan have the ability to engage in miracles? Scripture reveals that Satan has creaturely limitations but nevertheless is extremely powerful and influential in the world. He is called the "ruler of this world" (John 12:31), "the god of this world" (2 Corinthians 4:4), and the "prince of the power of the air" (Ephesians 2:2). He deceives the whole world (Revelation 12:9; 20:3) and has power in the governmental (Matthew 4:8-9), physical (Luke 13:11,16; Acts 10:38), angelic (Jude 9; Ephesians 6:11-12), and ecclesiastical (church) (Revelation 2:9; 3:9) realms.

Satan's Vast Experience

It is critical that Christians realize that Satan has vast experience in tricking human beings and bringing them down. In fact, his experience is far greater than that of any human being. By his very longevity, Satan has acquired a breadth of experience that easily eclipses the limited knowledge of man. He has observed people firsthand in every conceivable situation, so he can predict with accuracy how they will respond to circumstances. So although Satan is not omniscient, his wide experience gives him knowledge that is far superior to anything any human being could have.

Because of his vast experience, Satan has learned many wiles and tricks regarding how to deceive human beings. Some of his deceitful tricks no doubt relate to the counterfeit miracles he inspires. Christians are therefore urged to beware (2 Corinthians 2:11; 1 Peter 5:8).

Satan as the Ape of God

Augustine called the devil *Simius Dei*—"the ape of God." Satan is the great counterfeiter. He mimics God in many ways. A primary tactic Satan uses to attack God and His program in general is to offer a counterfeit kingdom and program. This is hinted at in 2 Corinthians 11:14, which makes reference to Satan masquerading as an angel of light.

In what ways does Satan act as the ape of God?

- Satan has his own church—the "synagogue of Satan" (Revelation 2:9).

- Satan has his own ministers of darkness—false prophets who bring false sermons (2 Corinthians 11:4-5).

- Satan has formulated his own system of theology, or "doctrines of demons" (1 Timothy 4:1; Revelation 2:24).

- Satan's ministers proclaim a counterfeit gospel (Galatians 1:7-8).

- Satan has his own throne (Revelation 13:2) and his own worshippers (13:4).

- Satan inspires false christs and self-constituted messiahs (Matthew 24:4-5).

- Satan employs false teachers who bring in destructive heresies (2 Peter 2:1).

- Satan sends out false prophets (Matthew 24:11).

All this mimicking indicates that Satan's plan has always been to establish and lead a rival rule to God's kingdom.

Scripture indicates that Satan performs counterfeit signs and wonders. Indeed, 2 Thessalonians 2:9 tells us, "The coming of the lawless one is by the activity of Satan with all power and false signs and wonders."

What About Miracles?

Though Satan has great spiritual powers, there is a gigantic difference between the power of the devil and the power of God. First, God is infinite in power (omnipotent); the devil is finite and limited. Second, only God can create life (Genesis 1:1,21; Deuteronomy 32:39); the devil cannot (see Exodus 8:19). Only God can truly raise the dead (John 10:18; Revelation 1:18).

Certainly the devil has great power to deceive people (Revelation 12:9), to oppress those who yield to him, and even to possess them (Acts 16:16). He is a master magician and a super scientist. And with his vast knowledge of God, man, and the universe, he is able to perform "false signs and wonders" (2 Thessalonians 2:9; see also Revelation 13:13-14). Simon the sorcerer in the city of Samaria amazed people with his Satan-inspired magic, but the miracles accomplished through

Philip were much, much greater (Acts 8:9-13). The devil's counterfeit miracles do not compete with God's true miracles.

Perhaps the best illustration of Satan's counterfeit wonders is found in the Exodus account. In Exodus 7:10, for example, we read that Moses's rod was turned into a snake by the power of God. Then, according to verse 11, Pharaoh "summoned wise men and sorcerers, and they, the magicians of Egypt, also did the same things by their secret arts." The purpose of these acts, of course, was to convince Pharaoh that his magicians possessed as much power as Moses and Aaron and that Pharaoh did not need to yield to their request to let Israel go. It worked, at least for the first three encounters (Aaron's rod, the plague of blood, and the plague of frogs). However, when Moses and Aaron, by the power of God, brought forth living lice from the sand, the magicians were not able to bring forth life (or living things). They could only exclaim, "This is the finger of God" (Exodus 8:19).

Biblical scholars differ as to whether Satan just does convincing tricks or genuine (albeit limited) miraculous works. Some scholars assert that the feats of Egypt's magicians, inspired by Satan, were done by sleight of hand. Perhaps the magicians had enchanted the snakes so that they became stiff and appeared to be rods. When cast down upon the floor, they came out of their trance and began to move as snakes. It is suggested that Satan, who is the "father of lies" (John 8:44), may have been pulling some kind of deceitful trick instead of performing a true miracle.

Other scholars say these were supernatural and miraculous acts of Satan who actually turned the rods of the magicians into snakes. Some believe the devil and demons may be able to perform some "grade B" miracles. As such, they may be capable of altering or manipulating the world's natural processes.

Still others believe Satan sometimes does tricks and sometimes does supernatural (albeit limited) miraculous works. Some of what he does is mere trickery, but some of what he does is supernatural. Remember that the devil showed the Lord Jesus all the kingdoms of the world in a moment of time (Luke 4:5) and is able to transform himself into an angel of light (2 Corinthians 11:14). These are obviously supernatural acts.

The question of whether Satan can perform miracles hinges on how one defines a miracle. If a miracle is any event that transcends physical causes in a limited way, then we can say Satan can do a miracle. If, however, we define a miracle as a supernatural act produced by the immediate power of God, then of course, Satan cannot do a miracle.

Whether Satan has the ability to perform a few limited grade-B miracles or whether his works are just impressive tricks, the scriptural evidence is undeniably clear that only God can perform heavy-duty grade-A miracles. Only God can fully control and supersede the natural laws He Himself created, though on one occasion He did grant Satan the power to bring a whirlwind on Job's family (Job 1:19). As the account of Job illustrates, all the power the devil has is granted him by God and is carefully limited and monitored (see Job 1:10-12). In other words, Satan is "on a leash." Satan's finite power is under the control of God's infinite power.

The Antichrist's Healing

In view of the scriptural evidence, we must conclude that in the end times, Satan will either perform a limited grade-B miracle in healing the antichrist or engage in some kind of masterful deception—or perhaps a combination of both. In any event, the world will be amazed that the mortal wound of the antichrist will be healed, and many will worship him. This will contribute to his ultimate goal of world dominion.

Satan Is Cast Out of Heaven

In Revelation 12:12-13 we find a sobering description of Satan's ousting from heaven, after which he indwells—or, at the very least, fully energizes—the antichrist: "Therefore, rejoice, O heavens and you who dwell in them! But woe to you, O earth and sea, for the devil has come down to you in great wrath, because he knows that his time is short!"

Notice the contrast between the "woe" and the rejoicing. Satan's access to heaven is hereby removed, and he will no longer be able to stand before the throne of God and accuse the brethren. For this there is rejoicing in heaven (see verses 10-12a).

Satan is filled with fury because he knows his time is short. More specifically, he knows his time is limited to a mere 1260 days—the last three and a half years of the tribulation period. This brings woe to the earth. Arnold Fruchtenbaum makes this note: "Because of Satan's wrath, it is woe for the earth. This is a very important point to note in the understanding of what is happening during the middle and second half of the tribulation."[7] In other words, things now go from bad to much, much worse on the earth. Thomas Constable writes, "Everyone living on the earth, especially believers, must beware because he now moves among them more antagonistically than ever."[8]

The World Church Is Destroyed

At this time, the antichrist, along with the ten kings who are under his authority, will destroy the false world church, the religious prostitute of the end times.

> The ten horns that you saw, they and the beast will hate the prostitute. They will make her desolate and naked, and devour her flesh and burn her up with fire, for God has put it into their hearts to carry out his purpose by being of one mind and handing over their royal power to the beast, until the words of God are fulfilled (Revelation 17:16-17).

The text gives no indicators or clues as to the precise timing of this event. However, it seems most logical and coherent to place it midpoint in the tribulation period, at the same time that the antichrist will assume the role of world dictator by proclamation (see Daniel 9:27; Matthew 24:15). It is logical to infer that at the same basic time, the antichrist will come into global dominion both politically and religiously, demanding even to be worshipped (Daniel 11:36-38; 2 Thessalonians 2:4; Revelation 13:8,15).

The beast and his allies will eventually throw off the harlot and thoroughly destroy her...This will probably occur in the middle of the Tribulation when Antichrist breaks his covenant with Israel and demands that everyone on earth worship him or die (Dan. 9:27; 11:26-38; Matt. 24:15; 2 Thess. 2:4; Rev. 13:8,15).[9]

The false religious system that flourished during the first half of the tribulation period will be obliterated because the antichrist will be on the religious center stage. The final world religion will involve worship of the antichrist alone. No competing religious systems will be allowed, including that of the Jews.

God's Two Prophetic Witnesses Are Executed and Resurrected

I previously noted that during the tribulation period, God will raise up two mighty witnesses who will testify to Him with astounding power. The miracles they perform are reminiscent of Elijah (1 Kings 17; Malachi 4:5) and Moses (Exodus 7–11).

These prophetic witnesses apparently emerge on the scene at the beginning of the tribulation period. They continue to minister for 1260 days, which is precisely three and a half years (the first half of the tribulation period). The two witnesses are then martyred by the antichrist.

When they have finished their testimony, the beast that rises from the bottomless pit will make war on them and conquer them and kill them, and their dead bodies will lie in the street of the great city that symbolically is called Sodom and Egypt, where their Lord was crucified. For three and a half days some from the peoples and tribes and languages and nations will gaze at their dead bodies and refuse to let them be placed in a tomb, and those who dwell on the earth will rejoice over them and make merry and exchange presents, because these two prophets had been a torment to those who dwell on the earth. But after the three and a half days a breath of life from God entered them, and they stood up on their feet, and great fear fell on those who saw them. Then they heard a loud voice from heaven saying to them, "Come up here!" And they went up to heaven in a cloud, and their enemies watched them (Revelation 11:7-12).

Notice several things here. First, the bodies of the witnesses lie lifeless in Jerusalem, and it is apparently by television and the Internet that people around the globe will gaze at them for three and a half days. Only modern technology can explain how the whole world will be able to watch all of this.

Notice also that the refusal to bury a corpse was, in biblical times, a way of showing contempt (see Acts 14:19; see also Deuteronomy 21:22-23). So God's two witnesses will be shown contempt with the whole world watching.

The people of the world will have something like a Christmas celebration when God's witnesses are put to death. They will exchange presents, apparently in relief that they are no longer around. As one expositor noted, "The only prophets people love are dead ones."[10]

But then something amazing happens. "A breath of life from God entered them, and they stood up on their feet, and great fear fell on those who saw them." The Christmas celebration quickly gives way to fear as people witness this mighty act of God. This resurrection and ascension of the two witnesses into heaven serves as a sobering exclamation point to their prophetic words throughout their three-year ministry.

Many will come to know the Lord during the tribulation period (Matthew 25:31-46; Revelation 7:9), so we can surmise that some of these conversions are likely due to the testimony and miracles of these witnesses.

The Antichrist Breaks His Covenant with Israel

Daniel 9:24-27 reveals that the event that will mark the beginning of the tribulation period is the signing of a covenant between the antichrist and Israel. We know it is the antichrist who does the signing, for verse 26 tells us that the signer will be "the prince who is to come." The antichrist will thus be the covenant maker, and he will come into power by heading up a revived Roman Empire (see Daniel 7:8).

Our text tells us that the antichrist "shall make a strong covenant with many for one week" (Daniel 9:27). This is a week of seven years, so the covenant the antichrist signs with Israel is designed to remain in effect for the full seven-year period. But the antichrist will double-cross Israel, for we are told that "for half of the week he shall put an end to sacrifice and offering." In other words, after the covenant has been in effect for three and a half years, he reneges on the covenant and causes Israel's temple sacrifices to cease.

Daniel 11:45 indicates that the antichrist will move from Europe into the land of Israel: "He shall pitch his palatial tents between the sea and the glorious holy mountain." Taking all this together, it seems clear that in the middle of the tribulation period, the antichrist will invade the holy land and cause sacrifices to cease in the Jewish temple.

Why cause the sacrifices to cease? The key reason is that near the midpoint of the tribulation period, the antichrist—having already attained political power—will now seek to assume religious power as well. Indeed, he will seek to cause the world to worship him (see 2 Thessalonians 2:4; Revelation 13:8). In order for him to be worshipped by all people on earth, he must necessarily destroy all competing religions—including the Jewish religion, with its Levitical sacrifices and offerings.

We can conclude that the antichrist starts out as Israel's protector but becomes Israel's persecutor. He turns from being Israel's defender to being its defiler.

The antichrist will become a defiler by setting up an image of himself in the Jewish temple—something prophetic Scripture calls the abomination of desolation.

The Abomination of Desolation Occurs

In the book of Daniel, the term "abomination of desolation" conveys the outrage or horror of a barbaric act of idolatry within God's holy temple (see the NASB rendering of 11:31; 12:11). Such an act utterly profanes and desecrates the temple.

Against this backdrop, we read this about the antichrist: "His armed forces will rise up to desecrate the temple fortress and will abolish the daily sacrifice. Then they will set up the abomination that causes desolation" (Daniel 11:31 NIV).

The New Testament adds further clarity on this abomination that causes desolation. It will apparently take place midway through the future tribulation period, when the antichrist—the "man of sin" (2 Thessalonians 2:4)—sets up an image of himself inside the Jewish temple (see Matthew 24:15).

This amounts to the antichrist enthroning himself in the place of deity, displaying himself as God (compare with Isaiah 14:13-14; Ezekiel 28:2-9). This blasphemous act will utterly desecrate the temple, making it abominable and therefore desolate. The antichrist—the world dictator—will then demand that the world worship and pay idolatrous homage to him. Any who refuse will be persecuted and even martyred. The false prophet, who is the antichrist's first lieutenant, will see to this.

An abomination took place on a lesser scale in 168 BC. Antiochus Epiphanies erected an altar to Zeus in the temple at Jerusalem and sacrificed a pig, an unclean animal, on it. Antiochus Epiphanies was thus a prototype of the future antichrist.

The fact that the antichrist will "abolish the daily sacrifice" in the Jewish temple is yet another indication of his self-exaltation. He will not allow competing systems of worship. No one is to be worshipped but him.

The False Prophet Carries Out His Diabolical Ministry

Revelation 13:13-15 pictures the false prophet as a beast and describes its work.

> It performs great signs, even making fire come down from heaven to earth in front of people, and by the signs that it is allowed to work in the presence of the beast [the antichrist] it deceives those who dwell on earth, telling them to make an image for the beast [the antichrist] that was wounded by the sword and yet lived. And it was allowed to give breath

to the image of the beast, so that the image of the beast might even speak and might cause those who would not worship the image of the beast to be slain.

As we have seen, Satan does not have the power to engage in the kind of grade-A miracles that God does. However, he can apparently perform lesser, grade-B miracles, and he empowers the false prophet to engage in these (see Exodus 7:11; 2 Timothy 3:8). The false prophet does this to induce people to worship Satan's substitute for Christ—the antichrist (see Daniel 9:27; 11:31; 12:11; Matthew 24:15).

One of the miraculous acts the false prophet accomplishes is animating an image of the beast in the Jewish temple. The apostle Paul earlier revealed that the antichrist himself will sit in God's temple (see 2 Thessalonians 2:4) and receive the worship that properly belongs only to God. Some prophecy scholars suggest that when the antichrist is not present in the temple, an image of him is placed there to provide an object of worship in his absence (see Revelation 13:14-15; 14:9,11; 15:2; 16:2; 19:20; 20:4).

Many wonder what is meant when Scripture affirms that the false prophet gives breath to the image of the beast so that it can even speak. One Bible expositor explains the verse this way:

> Only God is the Creator. So probably the beast's image is able to give an impression of breathing and speaking mechanically, like computerized talking robots today. There might be a combination of natural and supernatural powers to enable the beast out of the earth to accomplish his purpose.[11]

The false prophet may use some kind of scientific deception to appear to give breath to the image of the beast and enable it to speak. Do not forget that Satan has great intelligence and also has the limited ability to manipulate the forces of nature, as he did when he afflicted Job. So perhaps he is able to give the appearance of animating the image in some way. Whatever the explanation, many people on earth will be deceived by what they perceive to be supernatural.

This apparent animation sets the image of the beast apart from typical idols in Old Testament times. As we read in Psalm 135:15-16, "The idols of the nations are silver and gold, the work of human hands. They have mouths, but do not speak; they have eyes, but do not see." Likewise, Habakkuk 2:19 says, "Woe to him who says to a wooden thing, Awake; to a silent stone, Arise! Can this teach? Behold, it is overlaid with gold and silver, and there is no breath at all in it." Contrary to such dead idols, this idolatrous image of the antichrist will seem to be alive, even godlike.

The goal of these supernatural acts is to induce people around the world to worship the antichrist. The antichrist will put himself in the place of Christ, so he seeks worship, just as Jesus was worshipped many times during His three-year ministry on earth.

Recall also the scriptural command, "You shall worship no other god, for the LORD, whose name is Jealous, is a jealous God" (Exodus 34:14). Because the antichrist will demand worship, he will place himself in the position of deity.

The Antichrist Blasphemes God

The midpoint of the tribulation period seems to be when the antichrist engages in self-exaltation and self-deification. Second Thessalonians 2:4 says the antichrist "opposes and exalts himself against every so-called god or object of worship, so that he takes his seat in the temple of God, proclaiming himself to be God." There is no greater blasphemy than this. The antichrist truly is *anti*-Christ, putting himself in Christ's place.

This verse should be interpreted in conjunction with Revelation 13:5-6: "The beast was given a mouth uttering haughty and blasphemous words, and it was allowed to exercise authority for forty-two months. It opened its mouth to utter blasphemies against God, blaspheming his name and his dwelling, that is, those who dwell in heaven."

The beast will tolerate the worship of no one and nothing but himself. He places himself on center stage. He will set himself up on God's throne in the inner sanctuary of God's temple. Some people throughout church history have interpreted this to mean that the antichrist seeks to place himself on the throne of the human heart as an object of worship, but it would seem best to interpret Scripture literally, with the antichrist enthroning himself in the literal temple in Jerusalem. Many of the early church fathers took it this way, and there is no reason to depart from such a literal approach.

Many interpreters relate all this to the fall of Lucifer, which is recorded in Isaiah 14:13-14: "I will ascend to heaven; above the stars of God I will set my throne on high; I will sit on the mount of assembly in the far reaches of the north; I will ascend above the heights of the clouds; I will make myself like the Most High." Consider the implication of each of these statements.

- "I will ascend to heaven." Apparently Lucifer wanted to abide in heaven and desired equal recognition alongside God Himself.

- "Above the stars of God I will set my throne on high." The stars likely refer to the angels of God. Lucifer apparently desired to rule over the angelic realm with the same authority as God.

- "I will sit on the mount of assembly in the far reaches of the north." Scripture elsewhere indicates that the mount of assembly refers to the center of God's kingdom rule (see Psalm 48:2; Isaiah 2:2). The phrase is sometimes associated with the Messiah's future earthly rule in Jerusalem during the millennial kingdom. Satan may have desired to rule over human beings in place of the Messiah.

- "I will ascend above the heights of the clouds." Clouds often metaphorically represent the glory of God in the Bible (Exodus 13:21; 40:28-34; Job 37:15-16; Matthew 26:64; Revelation 14:14). Apparently Lucifer sought a glory equal to that of God Himself.

- "I will make myself like the Most High." Scripture says God possesses heaven and earth (Genesis 14:18-19). Apparently Lucifer sought the supreme position of the universe for himself. Satan wanted to exercise the authority and control in this world that rightfully belongs only to God. His sin was a direct challenge to the power and authority of God.

Remember that Lucifer, or Satan, energizes the antichrist. Just as Satan sought to set himself up as God in Isaiah 14, so the antichrist sets himself up as God. The antichrist will continue in this bogus divine role for 42 months—the last half of the tribulation period. And just as Lucifer was judged for being a pretender to the divine throne, so will the antichrist.

The Jewish Remnant Flees

The persecution of the Jews will escalate geometrically after Satan is cast out of heaven and down to the earth.

> When the dragon saw that he had been thrown down to the earth, he pursued the woman who had given birth to the male child. But the woman was given the two wings of the great eagle so that she might fly from the serpent into the wilderness, to the place where she is to be nourished for a time, and times, and half a time. The serpent poured water like a river out of his mouth after the woman, to sweep her away with a flood. But the earth came to the help of the woman, and the earth opened its mouth and swallowed the river that the dragon had poured from his mouth. Then the dragon became furious with the woman and went off to make war on the rest of her offspring, on those who keep the commandments of God and hold to the testimony of Jesus. And he stood on the sand of the sea (Revelation 12:13-17).

Who is the woman who becomes the object of Satan's great persecution?

> A woman clothed with the sun, with the moon under her feet, and on her head a crown of twelve stars...was

pregnant and was crying out in birth pains and the agony of giving birth…The dragon stood before the woman who was about to give birth, so that when she bore her child he might devour it. She gave birth to a male child, one who is to rule all the nations with a rod of iron, but her child was caught up to God and to his throne, and the woman fled into the wilderness, where she has a place prepared by God, in which she is to be nourished for 1,260 days (Revelation 12:1-6).

In this passage, the woman represents Israel, building on the Old Testament imagery of Israel as the wife of God (Isaiah 54:5-6; Jeremiah 3:6-8; 31:32; Ezekiel 16:32; Hosea 2:16). Consequently, the 12 stars represent the 12 tribes of Israel, and the moon may allude to God's covenant relationship with Israel because new moons are associated with covenant worship (1 Chronicles 23:31; 2 Chronicles 2:4; 8:13).

The male child refers to Jesus Christ. The dragon's attempt to devour the child likely alludes to Herod's massacre of male children (Matthew 2:13-18; see also Luke 4:28-29). The child was caught up to God in the sense that He ascended into heaven following His resurrection (Acts 1:9; 2:33; Hebrews 1:1-3; 12:2). The child—the divine Messiah—is destined to rule the nations (see Psalm 2:6-9).

In verses 12 and following, Satan seeks to persecute Israel with fury because he knows he has very little time left. But God provides supernatural aid, and the Jews manage to find shelter in a secret place.

> This hiding place was not clearly identified. Some suggest that it might be Petra, fortress capital of the Nabateans in Edom, south of the Dead Sea. This city has a narrow access which could easily be blocked but which opens up into a large canyon capable of caring for many thousands of people.[12]

The two wings probably refer to God's supernatural delivering power (see Exodus 19:4; Deuteronomy 32:11-12; see also Matthew 24:16; Mark 13:14; Luke 21:21).

Though God will preserve a remnant of Jews through this persecution, not all Jews will survive. Many prophecy scholars relate this passage to Zechariah 13:8, where we are prophetically told, "In the whole land, declares the LORD, two thirds shall be cut off and perish, and one third shall be left alive." Many will die, but a remnant will survive the onslaught.

Scripture informs us that God preserves the Jews for "a time, times, and half a time." This refers to the last three and a half years of the tribulation period (see Daniel 7:25; 12:7). This period also coincides with the 42 months referenced in Revelation 11:2 and 13:5. The last three and a half years of the tribulation period is often referred to as the great tribulation.

In the middle of the tribulation period, then, things become traumatic for the Jewish people in Jerusalem. The antichrist has assumed global political power, and now he declares himself to be God and exalts himself in the Jewish temple. To make matters worse, the antichrist is afire with a passion to persecute the Jewish people.

Jesus, in the Olivet Discourse, points to how bad things will be and predicts that Jews living in Jerusalem will flee for their lives.

> When you see the abomination of desolation spoken of by the prophet Daniel, standing in the holy place (let the reader understand), then let those who are in Judea flee to the mountains. Let the one who is on the housetop not go down to take what is in his house, and let the one who is in the field not turn back to take his cloak. And alas for women who are pregnant and for those who are nursing infants in those days! Pray that your flight may not be in winter or on a Sabbath. For then there will be great tribulation, such as has not been from the beginning of the world until now, no, and never will be (Matthew 24:15-21).

When these horrific circumstances unfold in Jerusalem, Jesus urges the Jews living there to have no concern whatsoever for personal belongings but rather to get out of town as quickly as possible. Time spent in gathering personal belongings might mean the difference between life and death. Jesus indicates that the distress is about to escalate dramatically and rapidly. Jeremiah 30:7 describes this as "a time of distress for Jacob." Jacob is another name for Israel.

Satan Makes War on the Saints

Scripture reveals that the antichrist will engage in great persecution against not only the Jews but also the saints of God during the tribulation period.

> [The beast] was allowed to make war on the saints and to conquer them. And authority was given it over every tribe and people and language and nation, and all who dwell on earth will worship it, everyone whose name has not been written before the foundation of the world in the book of life of the Lamb who was slain. If anyone has an ear, let him hear:
>
> > If anyone is to be taken captive,
> >   to captivity he goes;
> > if anyone is to be slain with the sword,
> >   with the sword must he be slain.
>
> Here is a call for the endurance and faith of the saints (Revelation 13:7-10).

A parallel passage is Daniel 7:21, which, speaking of the antichrist, tells us that he "made war with the saints and prevailed over them." Many will die. The Revelation passage tells us that the antichrist will conquer them, and the Daniel passage tells us he will prevail over them. There will be many martyrs during the future tribulation period.

"[The antichrist] makes war with God's people and overcomes many of them. They die rather than submit to him. His rule extends over all the world—the last world empire before Christ's Reign."[13] God's people would rather experience death, knowing that they will live forever with the true Christ, Jesus the divine Messiah.

The antichrist now exercises global dominion, with authority over every tribe, people, language, and nation. He is not only a political leader but also the central religious object of worship (2 Thessalonians 2:4). All who are on the earth—except for those whose names are recorded in the book of life—will pay homage to him.

What is the book of life? It is interesting to observe that the idea of a divine register containing names goes back as far as Moses's encounter with God on Mount Sinai (Exodus 32:32-33). The apostle Paul speaks of his fellow workers as those "whose names are in the book of life" (Philippians 4:3). The book of Revelation mentions the book of life six times (3:5; 13:8; 17:8; 20:12,15; 21:27). It contains the names of all those who belong to God. In Revelation 13:8 and 21:27, the book of life is said to belong specifically to the Lamb of God, Jesus Christ. Those whose names are not recorded in the Lamb's book of life will worship the antichrist.

Midtribulation Announcements Are Uttered from Heaven

Revelation 14 serves as a connecting link between the events that take place midway through the tribulation period (Revelation 10–13) and the events that transpire in the second half of the tribulation period (15–16). In Revelation 14, divine announcements...

- predict the failure of the program of the counterfeit trinity—Satan, the antichrist, and the false prophet
- announce the results of the approaching bowl judgments
- give words of assurance, encouragement, and comfort to the saints living in the second half of the tribulation[14]

Here are six key revelations from the heavenlies.

1. An angel "with an eternal gospel to proclaim to those who dwell on earth, to every nation and tribe and language and people" proclaims with a loud voice, "Fear God and give him glory, because the hour of his judgment has come, and worship him who made heaven and earth, the sea and the springs of water" (verses 6-7).

2. Another angel then proclaims, "Fallen, fallen is Babylon the great, she who made all nations drink the wine of the passion of her sexual immorality" (verse 8).

3. Yet another angelic proclamation follows. "If anyone worships the beast and its image and receives a mark on his forehead or on his hand, he also will drink the wine of God's wrath, poured full strength into the cup of his anger, and he will be tormented with fire and sulfur in the presence of the holy angels and in the presence of the Lamb. And the smoke of their torment goes up forever and ever, and they have no rest, day or night, these worshipers of the beast and its image, and whoever receives the mark of its name" (verses 9-11).

4. The apostle John then records an affirmation. "I heard a voice from heaven saying, 'Write this: Blessed are the dead who die in the Lord from now on.' 'Blessed indeed,' says the Spirit, 'that they may rest from their labors, for their deeds follow them!'" (verse 13).

5. Yet another angel appears with a proclamation. "Put in your sickle, and reap, for the hour to reap has come, for the harvest of the earth is fully ripe" (verse 15).

6. And yet another angel calls out from the altar. "Put in your sickle and gather the clusters from the vine of the earth, for its grapes are ripe" (verse 18).

Following these revelations from the heavenlies, the events of the second half of the tribulation period begin to transpire. Woe to those on earth!

The Second Half of the Tribulation

The Great Tribulation Begins

The events of the second half of the seven-year tribulation period are properly called the great tribulation. There are a number of reasons for making this distinction between the two halves of the tribulation period.

First, the foundational prophecy in Daniel 9:27 makes a distinction between the two halves. We read that the antichrist "shall make a strong covenant with many for one week, and for half of the week he shall put an end to sacrifice and offering." As we have seen, the week refers to a week of years, or seven years. For half of that week—that is, the last three and a half years—the antichrist will put an end to animal sacrifices in the Jewish temple.

The antichrist will do this because of his desire to be worshipped as God. Bible expositor Renald Showers explains: "By the middle of the 70th week, he will turn against every form of established worship to clear the way for the worship of himself. He will magnify himself to the level of deity."[1] He will take his seat in the Jewish temple, announce that he is God, and demand that his subjects worship him (see Daniel 11:36-37; 2 Thessalonians 2:3-4; Revelation 13:4-8,11-17; 19:20; 20:4).

In this context, the second half of Daniel 9:27 takes on great significance: "On the wing of abominations shall come one who makes desolate, until the decreed end is poured out on the desolator." Once the antichrist puts an end to the animal sacrifices in the Jewish temple at the midpoint of the tribulation period, he will apparently desolate the temple, and that desolation will apparently continue throughout the second half of the tribulation. This is one thing that makes this part of the tribulation so terrible—especially for the Jews.

Jesus warns the Jews to get out of Jerusalem quickly when the abomination of desolation occurs.

> When you see the abomination of desolation spoken of by the prophet Daniel, standing in the holy place (let the reader understand), then let those who are in Judea flee to the mountains. Let the one who is on the housetop not go down to take what is in his house, and let the one who is in the field not turn back to take his cloak. And alas for women who are pregnant and for those who are nursing infants in those days! Pray that your flight may not be in winter or on a Sabbath. For then there will be great tribulation, such as has not been from the beginning of the world until now, no, and never will be (Matthew 24:15-21).

The connection between this abomination of desolation and the beginning of the great tribulation, then, seems clear from a comparison of Daniel 9:27 with Matthew 24:15-21.

Speaking of this same time of travail, Daniel 12:1 comments, "there shall be a time of trouble, such as never has been since there was a nation till that time." This time period largely deals with Israel, so

Jeremiah 30:7 calls it "a time of distress for Jacob" (Jacob is a meta-phorical name referring to Israel). Truly this will be a time of great tribulation.

Time Limits of the Great Tribulation

These passages in Daniel and in Matthew's Gospel reveal the two defining characteristics of the great tribulation: the self-exaltation and forced worship of the antichrist, and his war against the people of God. By understanding how long the antichrist will be worshipped and how long he will persecute the saints, we can confirm that the great tribulation will last three and a half years.

The antichrist claims deity, blasphemes the one true God, and demands to be worshipped at the midpoint of the tribulation, and these activities continue for precisely three and a half years—that is, 42 months (Revelation 13:5). This confirms that the great tribulation will be the last three and a half years of the tribulation period.

Likewise, Daniel 7:25 reveals that the antichrist "shall wear out the saints of the Most High…and they shall be given into his hand for a time, times, and half a time"—three and a half years. The persecution of the saints is a defining characteristic of the great tribulation, so this verse confirms that the great tribulation will be the last three and a half years of the tribulation.

Yet another scriptural observation supports this view. We know that the antichrist's persecution of the saints begins at the midpoint of the tribulation (Revelation 13:5-10). This will continue until the "time came when the saints possessed the kingdom" (Daniel 7:21)—that is, until Jesus's second coming and the beginning of His millennial kingdom (see Zechariah 14:1-9; Revelation 19:11–20:6). Again, then, it would seem that the great tribulation will constitute the last three and a half years of the tribulation period.

Renald Showers quotes Irenaeus, the bishop of Lyons who lived during the second century and who supported this view.

> When this Antichrist shall have devastated all things in this world, he will reign for three years and six months, and sit

in the temple at Jerusalem; and then the Lord will come from heaven in the clouds, in the glory of the Father, sending this man and those who follow him into the lake of fire; but bringing in for the righteous the times of the kingdom.[2]

This being the case, how are we to understand these words of Jesus about the shortening of the great tribulation? "Then there will be great tribulation, such as has not been from the beginning of the world until now, no, and never will be. And if those days had not been cut short, no human being would be saved. But for the sake of the elect those days will be cut short" (Matthew 24:21-22). Was Jesus saying He would make the great tribulation shorter than three and a half years, or was He saying that three and a half years *is* the shortened time?

To answer this question, we turn to the parallel verse in Mark 13:20. "And if the Lord had not cut short the days, no human being would be saved. But for the sake of the elect, whom he chose, he shortened the days." Greek scholars note that the two verbs in this verse—"cut short" and "shortened"—express action that was taken by God in the past.

In this view, God in eternity past sovereignly decreed a limitation on the length of the great tribulation. What are God's sovereign decrees? Theologian Henry C. Thiessen tells us. "The decrees are God's eternal purpose. He does not make His plans or alter them as human history develops. He made them in eternity, and, because He is immutable, they remain unaltered (Ps. 33:11; James 1:17)."[3] (See also Isaiah 14:24-27; 46:9-11; Daniel 9:24,26-27; 11:36; Luke 22:22; Acts 2:23; 4:27-28; Ephesians 1:11; 3:11.)

In view of this, we conclude that Jesus was teaching that God in the past had already shortened the great tribulation. He did so in the sense that in the past He sovereignly decreed to cut it off at a specific time rather than let it continue indefinitely. In His omniscience, God knew that if the great tribulation were to continue indefinitely, all humanity would perish. To prevent that from happening, God in eternity past "sovereignly fixed a specific time for the Great Tribulation to end— when it had run its course for three and one-half years or 42 months or 1,260 days. *That fixed time cannot be changed.*"[4]

The Mark of the Beast

In Revelation 13, we read that the antichrist and the false prophet—a diabolical duo—will subjugate the entire world so that no one can buy or sell who does not receive the mark of the beast.

> [The false prophet] causes all, both small and great, both rich and poor, both free and slave, to be marked on the right hand or the forehead, so that no one can buy or sell unless he has the mark, that is, the name of the beast or the number of its name. This calls for wisdom: let the one who has understanding calculate the number of the beast, for it is the number of a man, and his number is 666 (verses 16-18).

Clearly, the book of Revelation reveals that the false prophet will seek to force human beings to worship the antichrist, the man of sin. He will require everyone to make a choice: Either receive the mark of the beast and worship the antichrist or starve, with no ability to buy or sell.

The next verse denotes a stark contrast. "Then I looked, and behold, on Mount Zion stood the Lamb, and with him 144,000 who had his name and his Father's name written on their foreheads." The antichrist's mark seems to be a parody of God's sealing of the 144,000 witnesses of Revelation 7 and 14. Prophecy experts Thomas Ice and Timothy Demy offer this suggestion: "God's seal of His witnesses most likely is invisible and for the purpose of protection from the antichrist. On the other hand, antichrist offers protection from the wrath of God—a promise he cannot deliver—and his mark is visible and external." They also note, "For the only time in history, an outward indication will identify those who reject Christ and His gospel of forgiveness of sins."[5]

Receiving this mark is a serious business, as we read in Revelation 14:9-10.

> If anyone worships the beast and its image and receives a mark on his forehead or on his hand, he also will drink the wine of God's wrath, poured full strength into the cup of his anger, and he will be tormented with fire and sulfur in

the presence of the holy angels and in the presence of the Lamb.

Revelation 16:2 pictures the scene. "The first angel went and poured out his bowl on the earth, and harmful and painful sores came upon the people who bore the mark of the beast and worshiped its image."

Such words are sobering. Any who express loyalty to the antichrist and his cause will suffer the wrath of our holy and just God. How awful it will be for these to experience the full force of God's divine anger and unmitigated vengeance (see Psalm 75:8; Isaiah 51:17; Jeremiah 25:15-16)!

Revelation 20:4 tells us, by contrast, that believers in the Lord Jesus Christ will refuse the mark of the beast. "I saw the souls of those who had been beheaded for the testimony of Jesus and for the word of God, and who had not worshiped the beast or its image and had not received its mark on their foreheads or their hands. They came to life and reigned with Christ for a thousand years."

What Is the Mark?

Apparently, people will somehow be branded, just as animals today are branded and as slaves were once branded by their slave owners. We cannot be certain how the number 666 relates to this personage or the mark. Bible interpreters have offered many suggestions as to the meaning of 666 down through the centuries. A popular theory is that inasmuch as 7 is the number of perfection, and the number 777 reflects the perfect Trinity, perhaps 666 points to a being who aspires to perfect deity (like the Trinity) but never attains it. (The antichrist is just a man, though influenced and possibly indwelt by Satan.)

Others have suggested that perhaps the number refers to a specific man—such as the Roman emperor Nero. It is suggested that if Nero's name is translated into the Hebrew language, the numerical value of its letters is 666. Some suggest that antichrist will be a man like Nero of old. Of course, all this is highly speculative. The truth is, Scripture does not clearly define what is meant by 666. Interpreting this verse involves some guesswork.

One thing is certain. In some way that is presently unknown to us, this number will be a crucial part of his identification. It is sobering to realize that receiving this mark of the beast is apparently an unpardonable sin (Revelation 14:9-10). The decision to receive the mark is an irreversible decision. Once made, there is no turning back.

Receiving the mark signifies approval of the antichrist and his purpose. No one takes this mark accidentally. One must choose to do so with all the facts on the table. The choice will be deliberate and have eternal consequences. Those who choose to receive the mark will do so with the full knowledge of what they have done.

The choice will cause a radical polarization. No middle ground is possible. One chooses either for or against the antichrist. One chooses either for or against God. People in our present day think they can avoid God and His demands on their lives by feigning neutrality, but no such neutrality will be possible during the tribulation, for one's very survival will be determined by a decision for or against God. One must choose to either receive the mark and live (being able to buy and sell) or reject the mark and face suffering and death. One must choose to follow antichrist and eat well or reject the antichrist and starve.

A Commerce Passport

The mark of the beast will be a commerce passport during the future tribulation period. Arnold Fruchtenbaum suggests that the mark of the beast will be given to all who submit themselves to the authority of the antichrist and accept him as god. "The mark will serve as a passport for business (Revelation 13:17a). They will be able to neither buy nor sell anything unless they have the mark…Only those who have this number will be permitted to work, to buy, to sell, or simply to make a living."[6]

This mark will apparently be required during the second half of the tribulation period. Prophecy scholar Mark Hitchcock suggests that there is ancient historical precedence for such a mark.[7] For example, he points to Ezekiel 9:4: "The LORD said to him, 'Pass through the city, through Jerusalem, and put a mark on the foreheads of the men who sigh and groan over all the abominations that are committed in it.'" This mark on the forehead preserved the faithful, just as the blood of the Passover Lamb marked the Israelites' doorposts and saved them from death during the final plague on the Egyptians (see Exodus 12:21-29).

Such a mark was also used in connection with pagans and false deities in ancient times, as Robert Thomas explains.

> The mark must be some sort of branding similar to that given soldiers, slaves, and temple devotees in John's day. In Asia Minor, devotees of pagan religions delighted in the display of such a tattoo as an emblem of ownership by a certain god. In Egypt, Ptolemy Philopator I branded Jews, who submitted to registration, with an ivy leaf in recognition of their Dionysian worship (cf. 3 Macc. 2:29). This meaning resembles the long-time practice of carrying signs to advertise religious loyalties (cf. Isa. 44:5) and follows the habit of branding slaves with the name or special mark of their owners (cf. Gal. 6:17). *Charagma* ("mark") was a [Greek] term for the images or names of emperors on Roman coins, so it fittingly could apply to the beast's emblem put on people.[8]

John MacArthur makes a similar note.

> In the Roman Empire, this was a normal identifying symbol, or brand, that slaves and soldiers bore on their bodies. Some of the ancient mystical cults delighted in such tattoos, which identified members with a form of worship. Antichrist will have a similar requirement, one that will need to be visible on the hand or forehead.[9]

Economy and Religion

Prophetic Scripture reveals that the false prophet will be an economic *and* religious leader. These two domains will become merged so that one depends on the other during the future tribulation. The mark of the beast will tie them together. David Jeremiah puts it this way:

"The mark will allow the Antichrist's followers to buy and sell because it identifies them as religiously orthodox—submissive followers of the Beast and worshippers of his image. Those without the mark are forbidden to buy because they are identified as traitors." So, though receiving the mark is essentially a spiritual decision, it will have life-and-death economic consequences.

High Technology Itself Is Not the Mark

This is a very important point. Though modern technology will enable the antichrist and false prophet to bring about a cashless society and control all commerce on earth, we must differentiate between this technology and the mark of the beast, for the technology itself is not the mark. I make this point because a number of prophecy expositors have claimed that the mark will be a high-tech chip inserted under the skin, a barcode on the hand or the forehead, some kind of universal product code, or some other such technology.

This is not the case. The mark itself will identify allegiance to the antichrist, but that is separate and distinct from the technology that enables him to enforce his economic system. John F. Walvoord comments on how technology will make it possible for such economical control, based on whether or not people have received the mark.

> There is no doubt that with today's technology, a world ruler, who is in total control, would have the ability to keep a continually updated census of all living persons and know day-by-day precisely which people had pledged their allegiance to him and received the mark and which had not.[10]

Dr. Walvoord also suggests, it is also highly likely that "chip implants, scan technology, and biometrics will be used as tools to enforce his policy that one cannot buy or sell without the mark."[11]

Notice that this mark will be *on* people, not *in* them (like some kind of micro computer chip). It will be on the right hand or head and will be visible (perhaps like a tattoo), not hidden beneath the skin. It will be universally rejected by God's people but universally accepted by unbelievers. Woe to those who receive the mark!

Deception Escalates

In Matthew 24:11, Jesus prophesies that in the tribulation period, "many false prophets will arise and lead many astray." The apostle Paul provides a similar teaching in 2 Thessalonians 2:9-11.

> The coming of the lawless one is by the activity of Satan with all power and false signs and wonders, and with all wicked deception for those who are perishing, because they refused to love the truth and so be saved. Therefore God sends them a strong delusion, so that they may believe what is false.

Notice that the lawless one (the antichrist) is energized and empowered by Satan. We learn from Scripture that Satan is the father of lies (John 8:44). Satan is a master deceiver and the greatest among all liars. His lies are typically religious, distorting the biblical picture of God, Jesus, and the true gospel.

Because Satan is the father of lies, the one whom he energizes—the antichrist—will also be characterized by lies and deception. The false signs and wonders that the antichrist performs will cause all the more deception because they will seem to exalt the antichrist as God among us.

Even worse, Satan will blind the minds of human beings so that they cannot perceive the truth. Second Corinthians 4:4 tells us that "the god of this world has blinded the minds of the unbelievers, to keep them from seeing the light of the gospel of the glory of Christ, who is the image of God."

Tragically, unbelievers during the tribulation period will have turned their backs on God, so God will hand them over to a powerful delusion. God desires all to be saved (1 Timothy 2:4-6), but many refuse God's truth and offer of salvation. When that happens, God eventually allows them to experience the full brunt of the consequences of falsehood (see Romans 1:18-25). The book of Revelation indicates that the unrepentant will experience those consequences during the second half of the tribulation, also known as the great tribulation.

The deception will be enormous. It seems to kick into highest gear at the midpoint of the tribulation. Scripture provides many evidences for this.

Revelation 12:9, for example, tells us that at the midpoint of the tribulation, "the great dragon was thrown down, that ancient serpent, who is called the devil and Satan, the deceiver of the whole world—he was thrown down to the earth, and his angels were thrown down with him." Once he is on the earth, he will either empower or indwell the antichrist to engage in deception.

In chapter 13, we are told that the false prophet carries out the bidding of the antichrist in engaging in deceptive acts. "By the signs that it is allowed to work in the presence of the beast it deceives those who dwell on earth, telling them to make an image for the beast that was wounded by the sword and yet lived" (Revelation 13:14). Many will fall for the deception.

This deception will finally end at the second coming of Christ. "The beast was captured, and with it the false prophet who in its presence had done the signs by which he deceived those who had received the mark of the beast and those who worshiped its image. These two were thrown alive into the lake of fire that burns with sulfur" (Revelation 19:20). Multitudes will suffer deception and receive the mark of the beast.

Satan will be bound during Christ's millennial kingdom "so that he might not deceive the nations any longer, until the thousand years were ended" (Revelation 20:3, see also verses 8,10). Deception will relentlessly flow from the satanic trinity—the antichrist, the false prophet, and Satan—during the great tribulation.

The Bowl Judgments

We earlier witnessed the unleashing of the seal judgments, involving bloodshed, famine, death, economic upheaval, a great earthquake, and severe cosmic disturbances (Revelation 6). We then witnessed the unleashing of the trumpet judgments, involving hail and fire mixed with blood, the sea turning to blood, water turning bitter, further cosmic disturbances, affliction by demonic scorpions, and the death of a third of humankind (Revelation 8:6–9:21).

Now, finally, the worst judgments of all fall on the earth during the great tribulation—the bowl judgments. A brief perusal of Revelation 16 reveals that these will be horrific days to be alive on the earth.

First bowl judgment. "The first angel went and poured out his bowl on the earth, and harmful and painful sores came upon the people who bore the mark of the beast and worshiped its image" (verse 2).

Second bowl judgment. "The second angel poured out his bowl into the sea, and it became like the blood of a corpse, and every living thing died that was in the sea" (verse 3).

Third bowl judgment. "The third angel poured out his bowl into the rivers and the springs of water, and they became blood. And I heard the angel in charge of the waters say, 'Just are you, O Holy One, who is and who was, for you brought these judgments. For they have shed the blood of saints and prophets, and you have given them blood to drink. It is what they deserve!'" (verses 4-6).

Fourth bowl judgment. "The fourth angel poured out his bowl on the sun, and it was allowed to scorch people with fire. They were scorched by the fierce heat, and they cursed the name of God who had power over these plagues. They did not repent and give him glory" (verses 8-9).

Fifth bowl judgment. "The fifth angel poured out his bowl on the throne of the beast, and its kingdom was plunged into darkness. People gnawed their tongues in anguish and cursed the God of heaven for their pain and sores. They did not repent of their deeds" (verses 10-11).

Sixth bowl judgment. "The sixth angel poured out his bowl on the great river Euphrates, and its water was dried up, to prepare the way for the kings from the east. And I saw, coming out of the mouth of the dragon and out of the mouth of the beast and out of the mouth of the false prophet, three unclean spirits like frogs. For they are demonic spirits, performing signs, who go abroad to the kings of the whole world, to assemble them for battle on the great day of God the Almighty. ('Behold, I am coming like a thief! Blessed is the one who stays awake, keeping his garments on, that he may not go about naked and be seen exposed!') And they assembled them at the place that in Hebrew is called Armageddon" (verses 12-16).

Seventh bowl judgment: The final bowl judgment is addressed in verses 17-21. However, because this judgment is unleashed in connection with the campaign of Armageddon, I will address it later.

Despite the horror of these woes from the hand of God, people will continue to harden their hearts. They will utterly refuse to repent and turn to God. Many of these will have fallen for the antichrist's deceptive promises and will end up in the lake of fire, like the antichrist and the false prophet.

And yet there is still time to repent and turn to God. As we are about to see, the gospel of the kingdom will be preached even in the midst of this pervasive rejection of God.

The Gospel of the Kingdom

Matthew 24:14 tells us that during the tribulation period, "this gospel of the kingdom will be proclaimed throughout the whole world as a testimony to all nations, and then the end will come." Even though persecution and affliction will be widespread, and even though many will harden their hearts against God, God will nevertheless have witnesses on earth who are committed to spreading His message about Jesus Christ and the coming kingdom.

Just as John the Baptist and Jesus in the Gospels often preached that the kingdom of God was near, so God's witnesses will do the same during the tribulation period. Jesus Christ will clearly be presented as the divine Messiah, the King who will rule in the coming kingdom. William MacDonald and Arthur L. Farstad note, "The gospel of the kingdom is the good news that Christ is coming to set up His kingdom on earth, and that those who receive Him by faith during the Tribulation will enjoy the blessings of His Millennial Reign."[12]

Those who turn to the King during the tribulation period will be granted entrance into Christ's thousand-year millennial kingdom, but those who reject the King will be forbidden entrance. Indeed, at the judgment that takes place following Christ's second coming, Christ will divide all people into two groups—sheep and goats (believers and unbelievers). The sheep (believers) will be invited into Christ's

millennial kingdom, but the goats (unbelievers) will be sent into punishment (see Matthew 25:31-46).

The book of Revelation makes it clear that many will respond to
this gospel of the kingdom. In the end, there will be "a great multitude
that no one could number, from every nation, from all tribes and peoples and languages, standing before the throne and before the Lamb,
clothed in white robes, with palm branches in their hands" (Revelation 7:9).

The End of the Tribulation

The Campaign of Armageddon Begins

Scripture reveals that human suffering will steadily escalate during the seven-year tribulation period. First are the seal judgments, involving bloodshed, famine, death, economic upheaval, a great earthquake, and cosmic disturbances (Revelation 6). Then come the trumpet judgments, involving hail and fire mixed with blood, the sea turning to blood, water turning bitter, further cosmic disturbances, affliction by demonic scorpions, and the death of a third of humankind (Revelation 8:6–9:21). Then come the bowl judgments, involving horribly painful sores on human beings, more bodies of water turning to blood, the death of all sea creatures, people being scorched by the sun, total darkness engulfing the land, a devastating earthquake, and much more (Revelation 16).

Worse comes to worst, however, when these already traumatized human beings are engaged in a catastrophic war campaign called Armageddon (see Daniel 11:40-45; Joel 3:9-17; Zechariah 14:1-3; Revelation 16:14-16). This takes place at the very end of the tribulation period. Millions of people will perish in the worst escalation of conflict ever to hit the earth.

The word Armageddon literally means "Mount of Megiddo" and refers to a location about 60 miles north of Jerusalem. This is the location of Barak's battle with the Canaanites (Judges 4) and Gideon's battle with the Midianites (Judges 7). This will be the site for the final horrific battles of humankind just prior to the second coming.

Napoleon is reported to have once commented that this site is perhaps the greatest battlefield he had ever witnessed. Of course, the battles Napoleon fought will dim in comparison to Armageddon. So horrible will Armageddon be that no one would survive if it were not for Christ coming again (Matthew 24:22).

Armageddon will involve an extended, escalating conflict, and it will be catastrophic. In view of all that occurs at Armageddon, it would be wrong to refer to it as a battle, as if it were a single event. We will see that the campaign of Armageddon actually involves eight phases.

Phase 1: The Antichrist's Allies Assemble for War

The allied armies of the antichrist will gather for the final destruction of the Jews. Demonic spirits "go abroad to the kings of the whole world, to assemble them for battle on the great day of God the Almighty...And they assembled them at the place that in Hebrew is called Armageddon" (Revelation 16:14,16).

The assembling of these armies actually takes place at the unleashing of the sixth bowl judgment. The Euphrates River will be dried up, thereby making it easier for the armies of the east to assemble. The Euphrates River—the longest river of Western Asia (almost 1800 miles)—begins in modern-day Turkey, heads toward the Mediterranean Sea, then turns south, flows more than 1000 miles, converges with the Tigris River, and then flows into the Persian Gulf. Many ancient cities, including Ur and Babylon, are located at various points along the river.

Who are the kings of the east? Bible scholars have varying opinions. In fact, a survey of 100 prophecy books reveals more than 50 different interpretations as to who they are. Some suggest that it may refer to the seven kings of Daniel 7 who have submitted to the authority of the antichrist. However, prophecy scholar John F. Walvoord suggests another interpretation.

> The simplest and best explanation, however, is that this refers to kings or rulers from the Orient or East who will participate in the final world war. In the light of the context of this passage indicating the near approach of the second coming of Christ and the contemporary world situation in which the Orient today contains a large portion of the world's population with tremendous military potential, any interpretation other than a literal one does not make sense.[1]

This is what makes the Euphrates River significant. This river is the primary water boundary between the Holy Land and Asia to the east. Theologian Charles Ryrie comments, "The armies of the nations of the Orient will be aided in their march toward Armageddon by the supernatural drying up of the Euphrates River." The drying up of this river is predicted in Isaiah 11:15.

The goal of the coalition will be to once and for all destroy the Jewish people. Each member of the satanic trinity will be involved—Satan, the antichrist, and the false prophet. Demons will also be involved in summoning the kings of the earth.

The summons will be reinforced by demonic activity to make sure that the nations will indeed cooperate in assembling their armies together. These demonic messengers will be empowered to perform signs in order to assure compliance and defeat any reluctance to fall into line on the part of the other kings.[2]

Phase 2: Commercial Babylon Is Destroyed

Revelation 17–18 reveals that the antichrist will rebuild and revive Babylon in the end times. It will be a worldwide economic and religious center. When the late Saddam Hussein was in power, he spent more than a billion dollars in oil money to rebuild the city, essentially as a monument to himself.

Earlier in the book, I noted that the antichrist will set up headquarters in Jerusalem halfway through the tribulation period, when he will claim to be God and set up an image of himself in the Jewish temple.

At some point in the latter half of the tribulation period—we are not told precisely when—the antichrist will shift his headquarters to Babylon, which will become a global commercial center. Babylon at this time will likely be in control of the oil fields (and the money these fields generate) in the Middle East. This Babylonian commercial center will be destroyed during phase 2 of Armageddon.

What an irony we have here. While phase 1 of Armageddon is underway, with the antichrist preparing his armies to attack Israel, God will cause a military force to attack the antichrist's headquarters of Babylon.

Several key passages describe the utter destruction of Babylon in association with Armageddon.

> Because of the wrath of the Lord she shall not be inhabited but shall be an utter desolation; everyone who passes by Babylon shall be appalled, and hiss because of all her wounds. Set yourselves in array against Babylon all around, all you who bend the bow; shoot at her, spare no arrows, for she has sinned against the Lord…
>
> How Babylon has become a horror among the nations! I set

a snare for you and you were taken, O Babylon, and you did not know it; you were found and caught, because you opposed the LORD. The LORD has opened his armory and brought out the weapons of his wrath...

As when God overthrew Sodom and Gomorrah and their neighboring cities, declares the LORD, so no man shall dwell there, and no son of man shall sojourn in her (Jeremiah 50:13-14,23-25,40).

Isaiah 13:19 informs us that Babylon "will be like Sodom and Gomorrah when God overthrew them." The book of Revelation is graphic in its description of commercial Babylon's destruction.

Then a mighty angel took up a stone like a great millstone and threw it into the sea, saying, "So will Babylon the great city be thrown down with violence, and will be found no more; and the sound of harpists and musicians, of flute players and trumpeters, will be heard in you no more, and a craftsman of any craft will be found in you no more, and the sound of the mill will be heard in you no more, and the light of a lamp will shine in you no more, and the voice of bridegroom and bride will be heard in you no more, for your merchants were the great ones of the earth, and all nations were deceived by your sorcery. And in her was found the blood of prophets and of saints, and of all who have been slain on earth" (Revelation 18:21).

Who will attack Babylon and the antichrist? A military coalition from the north.

For behold, I am stirring up and bringing against Babylon a gathering of great nations, from the north country. And they shall array themselves against her...

Behold, a people comes from the north; a mighty nation and many kings are stirring from the farthest parts of the earth. They lay hold of bow and spear; they are cruel and have no mercy. The sound of them is like the roaring of the

sea; they ride on horses, arrayed as a man for battle against
you, O daughter of Babylon! (Jeremiah 50:9,41-42).

Just as God used the Babylonians in Old Testament times as His rod
of judgment against Israel, so now God uses a northern coalition as His
whipping rod against Babylon. Just as Babylon showed no mercy in its
oppression of Israel, so God now shows no mercy to Babylon.

When Babylon is destroyed at the end of the tribulation period, the
antichrist will not be present in the city. He will be told of its destruction by messengers (see Jeremiah 50:43; 51:31-32). He becomes all the
more enraged.

Phase 3: Jerusalem Falls and Is Ravaged

Phase 2 of Armageddon involved the destruction of the antichrist's
capital of Babylon. However, even the destruction of his capital is not
enough to distract him away from his goal of destroying the Jewish
people. So instead of launching a counterattack against the northern
military coalition that wiped out Babylon, the antichrist and his forces
instead move south to attack Jerusalem. This constitutes phase 3 of
Armageddon. We read about it in Zechariah 12:1-3.

> Thus declares the LORD, who stretched out the heavens
> and founded the earth and formed the spirit of man within
> him: "Behold, I am about to make Jerusalem a cup of stag-
> gering to all the surrounding peoples. The siege of Jeru-
> salem will also be against Judah. On that day I will make
> Jerusalem a heavy stone for all the peoples. All who lift it
> will surely hurt themselves. And all the nations of the earth
> will gather against it."

Zechariah 14:2 adds this: "I will gather all the nations against Jerusalem to battle, and the city shall be taken and the houses plundered
and the women raped. Half of the city shall go out into exile, but the
rest of the people shall not be cut off from the city."

Notice that all the nations of the world gather against Jerusalem.
Sadly, many prophecy scholars believe this includes the United States.

Elsewhere in this book I noted the strong possibility that following the rapture of the church, the United States will likely become an ally of the revived Roman Empire—the United States of Europe.

In any event, with heavy losses on both sides, Jerusalem will fall and be ravaged in the face of this overwhelming attack force. The antichrist's armies gain initial victory. However, as we will see, Israel will soon attain ultimate victory through the direct intervention of its Messiah.

Phase 4: The Antichrist Moves South Against the Remnant

Not all of the Jews are in Jerusalem when the antichrist and his forces attack. Recall that in the middle of the tribulation period, the antichrist will break his covenant with Israel and exalt himself as deity, even putting an image of himself in the Jewish temple. Christ, in His Olivet Discourse, warns the Jews to flee for their lives as quickly as possible (Matthew 24:15-31). Many of the Jews apparently flee to the deserts and mountains (verse 16), perhaps in the area of Bozrah or Petra, about 80 miles south of Jerusalem. This escape from Jerusalem in described in Revelation 12.

> The woman [a metaphor referring to Israel] fled into the wilderness, where she has a place prepared by God, in which she is to be nourished for 1,260 days...The woman was given the two wings of the great eagle so that she might fly from the serpent into the wilderness, to the place where she is to be nourished for a time, and times, and half a time (verses 6,14).

The antichrist now targets this remnant of Jews. They sense impending doom as the forces of the antichrist gather in the rugged wilderness, poised to attack and annihilate them. From an earthly perspective, they are helpless and defenseless. This sets the stage for phase 5 of Armageddon.

Phase 5: Israel Endangered and Regenerated

The remnant of Israel is endangered and acutely aware that the forces of the antichrist have gathered to destroy them. However, the Jews' spiritual blindness is removed, and they call out to their Messiah, Jesus Christ, and experience national regeneration.

As a backdrop to understanding the significance of this, recall the words of the apostle Paul (himself a Jew who turned to the Messiah) in Romans 11:25: "I want you to understand this mystery, brothers: a partial hardening has come upon Israel, until the fullness of the Gentiles has come in." Paul also tells us, "Israel who pursued a law that would lead to righteousness did not succeed in reaching that law. Why? Because they did not pursue it by faith, but as if it were based on works. They have stumbled over the stumbling stone," which is Jesus Christ (Romans 9:31-32).

Put another way, Israel sought a relationship with God by means of a righteousness earned by keeping the law. Instead of seeking a faith-relationship with God through Christ, they instead sought to earn a relationship with God by doing everything that the law prescribed (see Galatians 2:16; 3:2,5,10).

Failure was unavoidable, for to attain righteousness by observing the law, the Jews would have had to keep it perfectly (James 2:10), which no man is capable of doing. To make matters worse, they refused to admit their inability to perfectly keep the law and turn by faith to God for His forgiveness. They rejected Jesus Christ as the Messiah, refusing to turn to Him in faith, because He did not fit their preconceived ideas about the Messiah (see, for example, Matthew 12:14,24). They "stumbled" over Him.

As a result, a partial judicial blindness or hardness of heart came upon Israel. Israel thus lost her favored position before God, and the gospel was then preached to the Gentiles so the Jews would become jealous and be saved (Romans 11:11). Israel's hardening and casting off is thus only temporary.

Now fast-forward to the campaign of Armageddon. The armies of the antichrist are gathered in the desert wilderness, poised to attack the Jewish remnant. At this desperate point, the Jews finally repent and turn to their divine Messiah.

Hosea 6:1-3 indicates that the Jewish leaders will call for the people of the nation to repent, and their collective repentance will take two days.

> Come, let us return to the LORD; for he has torn us, that he may heal us; he has struck us down, and he will bind us up. After two days he will revive us; on the third day he will raise us up, that we may live before him. Let us know; let us press on to know the LORD; his going out is sure as the dawn; he will come to us as the showers, as the spring rains that water the earth.

Whereas Jewish leaders once led the Jewish people to reject Jesus as their Messiah, now they urge repentance and instruct all to turn to Christ. This the remnant will do, and they will be saved.

This is in keeping with Joel 2:28-29, which informs us that there will be a spiritual awakening of the Jewish remnant. It would seem that Armageddon will be the historical context in which Israel finally becomes converted (Zechariah 12:2–13:1). In terms of chronology, the Israelites will confess their national sin (Leviticus 26:40-42; Jeremiah 3:11-18; Hosea 5:15) and then be saved, thereby fulfilling Paul's prophecy in Romans 11:25-27. In dire threat at Armageddon, Israel will plead for their newly found Messiah to return and deliver them (Zechariah 12:10; Matthew 23:37-39; see also Isaiah 53:1-9), and their deliverance will surely come (see Romans 10:13-14). Israel's leaders will have finally realized the reason why the tribulation has fallen on them—perhaps because the Holy Spirit will enlighten their understanding of Scripture, or because of the testimony of the 144,000 Jewish evangelists, or because of the testimony of the two prophetic witnesses.

It is sad to recognize that according to Zechariah 13:7-9, some two-thirds of the Jewish people will lose their lives during the tribulation period. However, one-third—the remnant—will survive, turn to the Lord, and be saved (see Isaiah 64:1-12).

Later, in the millennial kingdom, Israel will experience a full possession of the promised land and the reestablishment of the Davidic throne. It will be a time of physical and spiritual blessing, the basis of which is the new covenant (Jeremiah 31:31-34).

Phase 6: Jesus Christ Returns in Glory

The prayers of the Jewish remnant are answered! The divine Messiah returns personally to rescue His people from danger. The very same Jesus who ascended into heaven comes again at the second coming (Acts 1:9-11).

The second coming will involve a visible, physical, bodily return of the glorified Jesus. *Apokalupsis* is a key New Testament Greek word used to describe the second coming of Christ. It carries the basic meaning of "revelation," "visible disclosure," "unveiling," and "removing the cover" from something that is hidden. The word is used of Christ's second coming in 1 Peter 4:13: "Rejoice insofar as you share Christ's sufferings, that you may also rejoice and be glad when his glory is *revealed*."

Epiphaneia is another Greek word used of Christ's second coming in the New Testament. It means "to appear" or "to shine forth." In Titus 2:13 Paul speaks of "waiting for our blessed hope, the *appearing* of the glory of our great God and Savior Jesus Christ." In 1 Timothy 6:14 Paul urges Timothy to "keep the commandment unstained and free from reproach until the *appearing* of our Lord Jesus Christ."

The second coming will be a universal experience in the sense that every eye will witness the event. "Behold, he is coming with the clouds, and every eye will see him, even those who pierced him, and all the tribes of the earth will wail on account of him" (Revelation 1:7). Jesus referred to this as well. "Then will appear in heaven the sign of the Son of Man, and then all the tribes of the earth will mourn, and they will see the Son of Man coming on the clouds of heaven with power and great glory" (Matthew 24:30).

Moreover, in verse 29, Jesus explains that His return will be accompanied by magnificent signs in the heavens. Christ will come as the King of kings and Lord of lords with many crowns on His head— crowns that represent absolute sovereignty. His eyes will be like blazing fire (Revelation 19:11-16).

Old Testament prophetic Scripture reveals that Jesus returns first to the mountain wilderness of Bozrah, where the Jewish remnant is endangered (Isaiah 34:1-7; 63:1-6; Habakkuk 3:3; Micah 2:12-13). They will not be endangered for long!

Phase 7: The Final Battle Erupts

At Jesus' second coming, He will confront the antichrist and his forces and slay them with the word of His mouth. The description of the second coming in the book of Revelation makes it clear that the enemies of Christ suffer instant defeat.

> Then I saw heaven opened, and behold, a white horse! The one sitting on it is called Faithful and True, and in righteousness he judges and makes war. His eyes are like a flame of fire, and on his head are many diadems, and he has a name written that no one knows but himself. He is clothed in a robe dipped in blood, and the name by which he is called is The Word of God. And the armies of heaven, arrayed in fine linen, white and pure, were following him on white horses. From his mouth comes a sharp sword with which to strike down the nations, and he will rule them with a rod of iron. He will tread the winepress of the fury of the wrath of God the Almighty. On his robe and on his thigh he has a name written, King of kings and Lord of lords (Revelation 19:11-16).

And so instant deliverance comes to the Jewish remnant. The antichrist and his forces are poised for attack against the remnant in the wilderness. The remnant has no chance of survival. The Jewish leaders urge the remnant to repent and turn to Jesus the Messiah. That is when the second coming of Christ occurs.

Christ defeats all who stand against Israel. The antichrist will be slain. Habakkuk 3:13 prophesies of Christ's victory over the antichrist: "You went out for the salvation of your people, for the salvation of your anointed. You crushed the head of the house of the wicked, laying him bare from thigh to neck." Likewise, in 2 Thessalonians 2:8 we read of the antichrist, "whom the Lord Jesus will kill with the breath of his mouth and bring to nothing by the appearance of his coming."

The antichrist will be impotent and powerless in the face of the true Christ. All the forces of the antichrist will also be destroyed from Bozrah all the way back to Jerusalem (Joel 3:12-13; Zechariah 14:12-15; Revelation 14:19-20). What a wondrous day that will be.

Phase 8: Christ Victoriously Ascends to the Mount of Olives

In the final phase of the campaign of Armageddon, Jesus Christ victoriously ascends to the Mount of Olives. We read about this in Zechariah 14:3-4.

> Then the LORD will go out and fight against those nations as when he fights on a day of battle. On that day his feet shall stand on the Mount of Olives that lies before Jerusalem on the east, and the Mount of Olives shall be split in two from east to west by a very wide valley, so that one half of the Mount shall move northward, and the other half southward.

Then the seventh bowl judgment will be unleashed.

> The seventh angel poured out his bowl into the air, and a loud voice came out of the temple, from the throne, saying, "It is done!" And there were flashes of lightning, rumblings, peals of thunder, and a great earthquake such as there had never been since man was on the earth, so great was that earthquake. The great city was split into three parts, and the cities of the nations fell, and God remembered Babylon the great, to make her drain the cup of the wine of the fury of his wrath. And every island fled away, and no mountains were to be found. And great hailstones, about one hundred pounds each, fell from heaven on people; and they cursed God for the plague of the hail, because the plague was so severe (Revelation 16:17-21).

Clearly, when Christ ascends to the Mount of Olives, some cataclysmic events will bring an end to the tribulation period.

- An earthquake of globally staggering proportions (compare with Revelation 8:5 and 11:19). The whole earth will feel its effects. Mountains will be leveled. Islands will vanish. The topography of the earth will be drastically changed.

- Jerusalem will be split into three areas.

- The Mount of Olives will split into two parts, creating a valley.

- There will be a horrific hail storm, and the sun and moon will be darkened (see Joel 3:14-16; Matthew 24:29).

As these terrible events subside, the tribulation period finally comes to a close. But judgments nevertheless remain on the horizon—the judgment of the nations (Matthew 25:31-46) and the judgment of Israel (Ezekiel 20). Both of these judgments precede Christ's millennial kingdom.

After the Tribulation, Before the Millennial Kingdom

A 75-Day Transitional Period

A 75-day interval apparently separates the end of the tribulation period from the beginning of the millennial kingdom. During this brief interim, a number of significant events transpire.

For example, the image of the antichrist that had caused the abomination of desolation at the midpoint of the tribulation will be removed from the temple after 30 days. "From the time that the regular burnt offering is taken away and the abomination that makes desolate is set up, there shall be 1,290 days" (Daniel 12:11). The last half of the tribulation lasts only 1260 days (or three and a half years), so the abomination that makes desolate is removed from the Jewish temple 30 days after the tribulation ends.

An additional 45 days must also be added into the prophetic

timetable: "Blessed is he who waits and arrives at the 1,335 days" (verse 12). The 1335 days minus the 1290 days means another 45 days are added into the mix. Apparently, this is when the judgment of the nations takes place (Matthew 25:31-46). The Jewish survivors of the tribulation period will also be judged.

Other key events probably take place during this interval. Here are six.

1. The antichrist and the false prophet will be cast into the lake of fire. "The beast was captured, and with it the false prophet who in its presence had done the signs by which he deceived those who had received the mark of the beast and those who worshiped its image. These two were thrown alive into the lake of fire that burns with sulfur" (Revelation 19:20).

It is interesting to observe that the great white throne judgment, in which wicked human beings are judged and then cast into the lake of fire, does not occur until after the millennial kingdom. This means that for a full 1000 years, the antichrist and the false prophet will be the only inhabitants of the lake of fire. They will have plenty of time to ponder the futility of their efforts.

2. Satan will also be bound from this point till the very end of the millennial kingdom.

> Then I saw an angel coming down from heaven, holding in his hand the key to the bottomless pit and a great chain. And he seized the dragon, that ancient serpent, who is the devil and Satan, and bound him for a thousand years, and threw him into the pit, and shut it and sealed it over him, so that he might not deceive the nations any longer (Revelation 20:1-3).

3. Old Testament saints will be resurrected from the dead. "Your dead shall live; their bodies shall rise. You who dwell in the dust, awake and sing for joy! For your dew is a dew of light, and the earth will give birth to the dead" (Isaiah 26:19). "Many of those who sleep in the dust of the earth shall awake, some to everlasting life, and some to shame and everlasting contempt" (Daniel 12:2).

4. Finally, tribulation saints who had died are resurrected from the dead. "I saw the souls of those who had been beheaded for the testimony of Jesus and for the word of God, and those who had not worshiped the beast or its image and had not received its mark on their foreheads or their hands. They came to life and reigned with Christ for a thousand years" (Revelation 20:4).

5. Renald Showers suggest that the governmental structure of the coming millennial kingdom will be set up during these extra 45 days. Scripture reveals that the saints will reign with Christ in the millennial kingdom (2 Timothy 2:12; Revelation 20:4-6). Showers notes, "After the saints and unbelievers have been separated and the unbelievers are removed in judgment, it will take time to appoint saints to different government positions and inform them of their various responsibilities."[1]

6. It is also entirely feasible that the marriage feast of Christ, the divine Bridegroom, and His bride, the church, will take place at the close of the 75-day period. If so, it will be the highlight of that two-and-a-half-month period. The invitation to the marriage feast was previously mentioned in Revelation 19:9 (which just precedes the second coming): "Blessed are those who are invited to the marriage supper of the Lamb." It would thus make sense that the marriage feast would take place shortly after.

Following the 75-day interval, Christ will set up His millennial kingdom (Isaiah 2:2-4; Ezekiel 37:1-13; 40–48; Micah 4:1-7; Revelation 20). Before discussing this glorious kingdom, however, let's consider further details on the judgment of the nations, the judgment of the Jews, and the marriage feast of Jesus the Bridegroom and His bride, the church.

The Judgment of the Nations

Matthew 25:31-46 describes the judgment of the nations, which takes place following the second coming of Christ. The nations are comprised of the sheep and the goats, representing the saved and the lost among the Gentiles. According to Matthew 25:32, they are intermingled and require separation by a special judgment.

Some interpreters have argued that this judgment is the same as the great white throne judgment in Revelation 20:11-13, a judgment that takes place at the end of the millennial kingdom. However, a comparison of the judgment in Matthew with the one in Revelation makes this view impossible.

The Judgment of the Nations Matthew 25:31-46	The Great White Throne Judgment Revelation 20:11-15
occurs at the second coming	occurs after the millennial kingdom
occurs on earth	occurs at the great white throne
includes the sheep, the goats, and the brothers	includes the unsaved dead of all time
based on treatment of Christ's brothers	based on works
The righteous enter the kingdom, and the unrighteous are cast into the lake of fire.	The unsaved dead are cast into the lake of fire (none of the saved are present).
No resurrection is mentioned.	The unsaved dead are resurrected to be judged.

Clearly, a plain reading of the text indicates that these judgments are not the same. The judgment of the nations deals with the Gentile nations and takes place following the second coming of Christ.

Relation to Buying and Selling

During the tribulation period, people will not be able to buy or sell if they don't receive the mark of the beast (Revelation 13:16-17). Christians will need to act sacrificially toward those who are less fortunate.

> When the Son of Man comes in his glory, and all the angels with him, then he will sit on his glorious throne. Before him will be gathered all the nations, and he will separate people one from another as a shepherd separates the sheep

from the goats. And he will place the sheep on his right, but the goats on the left. Then the King will say to those on his right, "Come, you who are blessed by my Father, inherit the kingdom prepared for you from the foundation of the world. For I was hungry and you gave me food, I was thirsty and you gave me drink, I was a stranger and you welcomed me, I was naked and you clothed me, I was sick and you visited me, I was in prison and you came to me." Then the righteous will answer him, saying, "Lord, when did we see you hungry and feed you, or thirsty and give you drink? And when did we see you a stranger and welcome you, or naked and clothe you? And when did we see you sick or in prison and visit you?" And the King will answer them, "Truly, I say to you, as you did it to one of the least of these my brothers, you did it to me."

Then he will say to those on his left, "Depart from me, you cursed, into the eternal fire prepared for the devil and his angels. For I was hungry and you gave me no food, I was thirsty and you gave me no drink, I was a stranger and you did not welcome me, naked and you did not clothe me, sick and in prison and you did not visit me." Then they also will answer, saying, "Lord, when did we see you hungry or thirsty or a stranger or naked or sick or in prison, and did not minister to you?" Then he will answer them, saying, "Truly, I say to you, as you did not do it to one of the least of these, you did not do it to me." And these will go away into eternal punishment, but the righteous into eternal life (Matthew 25:31-46).

Notice the basis of the judgment of these Gentile peoples. One's destiny—entering Christ's kingdom or entering into punishment—hinges on how one treated Christ's brothers.

Who are these brothers? A comparison of this passage with the details of the tribulation recorded in Revelation 4–19 suggests the possibility that the term *brothers* may be referring to the 144,000 Jews mentioned in Revelation 7, Christ's Jewish brothers who bear witness of Him during the tribulation. Bible expositor Stan Toussaint, one of my former professors at Dallas Theological Seminary, notes, "It seems best to say that 'brothers of Mine' is a designation of the godly remnant of Israel that will proclaim the gospel of the kingdom unto every nation of the world."[2] Bible expositor Merrill F. Unger agrees.

> During the tribulation period, God will sovereignly call and save 144,000 Jews…So glorious and wonderful will be the ministry of the 144,000 saved Jews and so faithful will be their powerful testimony, the King on His throne of glory will not be ashamed to call them "My brothers." More than that, He will consider Himself so intimately united to them that what was done or not done to them is the same as being actually done or not done to Himself.[3]

Bible expositor J. Dwight Pentecost likewise notes that the 144,000 Jews…

> will be under a death sentence by the beast. They will refuse to carry the beast's mark, and so they will not be able to buy and sell. Consequently, they will have to depend on those to whom they minister for hospitality, food, and support. Only those who receive the message will jeopardize their lives by extending hospitality to the messengers. Therefore what is done for them will be an evidence of their faith in Christ, that is, what is done for them will be done for Christ.[84]

The *Bible Knowledge Commentary* provides this summary.

> The expression "these brothers" must refer to a third group that is neither sheep nor goats. The only possible group would be Jews, physical brothers of the Lord. In view of the distress in the Tribulation period, it is clear that any believing Jew will have a difficult time surviving (cf. 24:15-21). The forces of the world dictator will be doing everything possible to exterminate all Jews (cf. Rev. 12:17). A Gentile going out of his way to assist a Jew in the Tribulation will

mean that Gentile has become a believer in Jesus Christ during the Tribulation. By such a stand and action, a believing Gentile will put his life in jeopardy. His works will not save him; but his works will reveal that he is redeemed.[5]

Here, then, is the main point: The antichrist and the false prophet will wield economical control over the world during the tribulation period (Revelation 13), but God will still be at work. His redeemed will come to the aid of Christ's Jewish brethren as they bear witness to Christ all around the world. These will be invited into Christ's millennial kingdom.

These saved Gentiles are not yet given resurrection bodies. They will enter the kingdom in their mortal bodies and continue to have babies throughout the millennium (just as their Jewish counterparts will—see next chapter). Though longevity will characterize the millennial kingdom, both mortal Jews and Gentiles will continue to age and die (see Isaiah 65:20). They will be resurrected at the end of the millennium (Revelation 20:4-5). (More on this later in the book.)

The Judgment of the Jews

The judgment of the Jews is described in Ezekiel 20:34-38 (see also Matthew 25:1-30).

> I will bring you out from the peoples and gather you out of the countries where you are scattered, with a mighty hand and an outstretched arm, and with wrath poured out. And I will bring you into the wilderness of the peoples, and there I will enter into judgment with you face to face. As I entered into judgment with your fathers in the wilderness of the land of Egypt, so I will enter into judgment with you, declares the Lord GOD. I will make you pass under the rod, and I will bring you into the bond of the covenant. I will purge out the rebels from among you, and those who transgress against me. I will bring them out of the land where they sojourn, but they shall not enter the land of Israel. Then you will know that I am the LORD.

Here are four important facts about this judgment.

- It will take place after the Lord has gathered the Israelites from all around the earth to Palestine.

- Christ will purge out the rebels—those who have refused to turn to Him for salvation.

- Believers from among this group will enter into Christ's millennial kingdom, where they will then enjoy the blessings of the new covenant (verse 37; see also Jeremiah 31:31).

- These saved Jews are not yet given resurrection bodies. They will enter the kingdom in their mortal bodies and continue to have babies throughout the millennium (just as their Gentile counterparts will). Though longevity will characterize the millennial kingdom, both mortal Jews and Gentiles will continue to age and die (Isaiah 65:20). They will be resurrected at the end of the millennium (Revelation 20:4). (More on this later in the book.)

The Marriage Supper of the Lamb

Earlier in the book, I noted that Scripture describes the relationship between Christ and the church as a marriage. Christ is the Bridegroom, and the church is the bride. Jesus Christ, the Lamb, frequently referred to Himself as a Bridegroom (see Matthew 9:15; 22:2-14; 25:1-13; Mark 2:19-20; Luke 5:34-35; 14:15-24; John 3:29). The church is regarded as a virgin bride awaiting the coming of her heavenly Bridegroom (2 Corinthians 11:2). While she waits, she keeps herself pure, unstained from the world.

> Let us rejoice and exult and give him the glory, for the marriage of the Lamb has come, and his Bride has made herself ready; it was granted her to clothe herself with fine linen, bright and pure—for the fine linen is the righteous deeds of the saints.
>
> And the angel said to me, "Write this: Blessed are those

who are invited to the marriage supper of the Lamb." And he said to me, "These are the true words of God" (Revelation 19:7-9).

As we saw in chapters 3 and 5, Hebrew weddings included three phases: The bride became betrothed to the bridegroom, the bridegroom came to claim his bride, and the marriage supper was celebrated—a feast lasting up to a week. All three of these phases are seen in Christ's relationship to the church, the bride of Christ.

First, as individuals living during the church age come to salvation, they become a part of the church, the bride of Christ, betrothed to the divine Bridegroom.

Second, the Bridegroom (Jesus Christ) comes to claim His bride at the rapture, at which time He takes the bride to heaven, the Father's house, where He has prepared a place to live (John 14:1-3). The actual marriage takes place in heaven, sometime after the church has been raptured, prior to the second coming (Revelation 19:11-16). The bride is dressed beautifully in fine linen (verses 8,14).

Third, the marriage supper of the Lamb apparently takes place on earth during the 75-day interval between the end of the tribulation period and the beginning of the millennial kingdom.

During the Millennial Kingdom

The Millennial Kingdom Begins

Following the second coming of Christ, Jesus will personally set up His kingdom on earth. In theological circles, this is known as the millennial kingdom (Revelation 20:2-7; see also Psalm 2:6-9; Isaiah 65:18-23; Jeremiah 31:12-14,31-37; Ezekiel 34:25-29; 37:1-13; 40–48; Daniel 2:35; 7:13-14; Joel 2:21-27; Amos 9:13-14; Micah 4:1-7; Zephaniah 3:9-20).

In the chronology of the book of Revelation, the millennial kingdom clearly follows the second coming of Jesus Christ. Revelation 19 and 20 are chronological, with the second coming described in chapter 19 and the millennial kingdom described in chapter 20. The second coming lays a foundation for the establishment of the millennial kingdom. John Walvoord explains that the second coming…

> includes the destruction of the armies gathered against God in the Holy Land (Revelation 19:17,21), the capture of the Beast and the False Prophet and their being cast into the lake of fire (v. 20), the binding of Satan (20:1-3), and the resurrection of the martyred dead of the tribulation to reign with Christ a thousand years (vv. 4-6). A literal interpretation of Revelation 20:4-6 requires that Christ reign on earth for a thousand years following his second coming.[1]

The Tribulation Saints Enter the Millennial Kingdom

We have seen that following the second coming of Christ, the Gentiles will face Christ at the judgment of the nations (Matthew 25:31-46). Only believers will be invited into Christ's millennial kingdom in their mortal bodies (verses 34,46). Likewise, the redeemed remnant among the Jews will be invited to enter into the millennial kingdom in their mortal bodies (Ezekiel 20:34-38).

Though longevity will characterize the millennial kingdom, Scripture reveals that both mortal Jews and Gentiles will continue to age and die (Isaiah 65:20). Scripture also reveals that married couples among both groups will continue to have children throughout the millennium. All who die during this time will be resurrected at the end of the millennium (Revelation 20:4-5).

Some Bible interpreters in recent days—Robert Gundry is one example—have suggested that both saved *and* unsaved people will enter into Christ's 1000-year millennial kingdom. Such a view, however, does not fit the facts of biblical prophecy.

The Bible clearly indicates that only saved people enter the millennium, and the wicked are cut off (see Isaiah 1:19-28; 65:11-12; 66:15-16;

Jeremiah 25:27-33; 30:23-24; Ezekiel 11:21; 20:33-44; Micah 5:9-15; Zechariah 13:9; Malachi 3:2-6,18; 4:3). Isaiah 60:21 seems explicit: "Your people shall *all be righteous*; they shall possess the land forever, the branch of my planting, the work of my hands, that I might be glorified" (see also Isaiah 26:2).

Scripture reveals that Gentiles will definitely enter into Christ's millennial kingdom, but they will be converted prior to their admission (see Isaiah 16:5; 18:7; 19:19-21; 23:17-18; 55:5-6; 56:6-8; 60:3-5; 61:8-9; Jeremiah 3:17; 16:19-21; Amos 9:12; Obadiah 17-21). Moreover, Scripture positively states that they will be in subjection to the Messiah (Isaiah 42:1; 49:6; Zechariah 8:22-23).

Daniel's prophetic book also informs us that only the saints enter into God's kingdom. We are told that "the saints of the Most High shall receive the kingdom and possess the kingdom…The time came when the saints possessed the kingdom" (Daniel 7:18,22). The word *saint* in Daniel is from an Aramaic word that is derived from a Hebrew root *oilp*. This word has the connotation of a divine claim and ownership of the person. It connotes that which is distinct from the common or profane. In other words, profane people do not enter into the millennial kingdom. Only those who are God's people—those "owned" by God—enter in.

Further, it seems inconceivable that the wicked and the saints could together inherit a kingdom universally characterized by righteousness (Isaiah 61:11), peace (Isaiah 2:4), holiness (Isaiah 4:3-4), and justice (Isaiah 9:7). The parable of the wheat and tares (Matthew 13:30-31) and the parable of the good and bad fish (Matthew 13:49-50) confirm that only the saved go into the kingdom.

Of course, the fact that only saints enter into the kingdom does not stand against the possibility that some of the children of the saints will not be believers. After a few years have passed there will be people, born during the early days of the millennium, who will grow to adulthood rejecting the Savior-King in their hearts (though outwardly obeying Him). Some of these will eventually participate in the final revolt against God that takes place at the end of the millennium under Satan's lead (who is released from the abyss after the thousand years).

Israel Is Restored and Possesses the Land

Jeremiah 31:31-34, a pivotal prophecy dealing with the new covenant, promises the regeneration of Israel.

> Behold, the days are coming, declares the LORD, when I will make a new covenant with the house of Israel and the house of Judah, not like the covenant that I made with their fathers on the day when I took them by the hand to bring them out of the land of Egypt, my covenant that they broke, though I was their husband, declares the LORD. But this is the covenant that I will make with the house of Israel after those days, declares the LORD: I will put my law within them, and I will write it on their hearts. And I will be their God, and they shall be my people. And no longer shall each one teach his neighbor and each his brother, saying, "Know the LORD," for they shall all know me, from the least of them to the greatest, declares the LORD. For I will forgive their iniquity, and I will remember their sin no more.

This covenant promises the necessary internal power for the Jews to obey God's commands—something the Mosaic covenant of the law could never accomplish. This covenant promises a complete national regeneration of Israel, and every Jew in the millennial kingdom will personally know the Lord (see Isaiah 29:22-24; 30:18-22; 44:1-5; 45:17; Jeremiah 24:7; 50:19-20; Ezekiel 11:19-20; 36:25-27; Hosea 1:10–2:1; 14:4-8; Joel 2:28-32; Micah 7:8-20; Zephaniah 3:9-13; Romans 11:25-27).

Israel will not only experience regeneration in fulfillment of the new covenant (Jeremiah 31:31-34) but also be regathered. The land covenant recorded in Deuteronomy 29–30 is eternal and unconditional. God promised that even though Israel would be dispersed all over the world, He would gather them and restore them to the land (see Isaiah 43:5-7; Jeremiah 16:14-18). This will take place in Christ's millennial kingdom.

This is highly significant from a prophetic standpoint. God long ago made specific land promises to Abraham.

On that day the LORD made a covenant with Abram and said, "To your descendants I give this land, from the Wadi of Egypt to the great river, the Euphrates—the land of the Kenites, Kenizzites, Kadmonites, Hittites, Perizzites, Rephaites, Amorites, Canaanites, Girgashites and Jebusites" (Genesis 15:18-21 NIV).

God passed these land promises down to Isaac and his descendants.

Stay in this land for a while, and I will be with you and will bless you. For to you and your descendants I will give all these lands and will confirm the oath I swore to your father Abraham. I will make your descendants as numerous as the stars in the sky and will give them all these lands, and through your offspring all nations on earth will be blessed (Genesis 26:3-4 NIV).

God also reiterated the land promises to Jacob and his descendants.

I am the LORD, the God of your father Abraham and the God of Isaac. I will give you and your descendants the land on which you are lying. Your descendants will be like the dust of the earth, and you will spread out to the west and to the east, to the north and to the south. All peoples on earth will be blessed through you and your offspring (Genesis 28:13-14 NIV).

The Bible later affirmed that God's covenant promises would be fulfilled through this distinct family line.

He remembers his covenant forever, the promise he made, for a thousand generations, the covenant he made with Abraham, the oath he swore to Isaac. He confirmed it to Jacob as a decree, to Israel as an everlasting covenant: "To you I will give the land of Canaan as the portion you will inherit" (Psalm 105:8-11 NIV).

It is clear, then, that after God gathers the Jews from around the world, they will finally and completely come into full possession of the land that God promised them. The fulfillment comes thousands of years after the promise was initially made, but God is utterly faithful. Israel will be in full possession of the land just as God said they would be. This will happen at the beginning of Christ's millennial kingdom.

A Millennial Temple Is Built

In Ezekiel 40–48, a millennial temple is built (see Isaiah 2:3; 60:13; Joel 3:18) and millennial animal sacrifices are instituted (see Isaiah 56:7; 60:7; Jeremiah 33:17-18; Zechariah 14:19-21). Scholars have debated the question about whether these prophecies should be taken literally or in some figurative sense.

Some interpret the chapters symbolically, suggesting that the temple is somehow representative of the church. The problem is, those who see it as representative of the church do not agree among themselves what the symbol is supposed to say about the church. Because the text reads quite literally, providing precise dimensions, specifications, and instructions (just as specific as those for the tabernacle and the temple of Solomon), it seems obvious to the unbiased interpreter that the passage is intended to be taken literally—that is, there will in fact be a millennial temple and millennial animal sacrifices. Further, in view of the fact that Ezekiel was told, "Declare all that you see *to the house of Israel*" (Ezekiel 40:4), it seems impossible to conclude that this is supposed to symbolize the future church.

The millennial temple will be the final temple for Israel. The dimensions provided for this temple make it significantly larger than the three other temples built in Israel's history (Solomon's temple, the postexilic temple, and the tribulation temple).

This large temple will apparently represent God's presence among His people during the millennium (see Ezekiel 37:26-27). The restoration of Israel as a nation will appear to include a restoration of God's presence (and glory) visibly reentering the temple and being with His people. This temple will be a worship center of Jesus Christ during the entire millennium. It will be built at the beginning of the messianic kingdom (Ezekiel 37:26-28) by Christ (Zechariah 6:12-13), redeemed

Jews (Ezekiel 43:10-11), and representatives from the Gentile nations (Haggai 2:7; Zechariah 6:15).

Ezekiel 37:26-28 describes this temple as God's dwelling place among the people:

> I will make a covenant of peace with them. It shall be an everlasting covenant with them. And I will set them in their land and multiply them, and will set my sanctuary in their midst forevermore. My dwelling place shall be with them, and I will be their God, and they shall be my people. Then the nations will know that I am the LORD who sanctifies Israel, when my sanctuary is in their midst forevermore.

Even redeemed Gentiles will be included in worship in this millennial temple (see Isaiah 60:6; Zephaniah 3:10; Zechariah 2:11). The worship of Jesus Christ in the future temple is a key aspect of divine revelation on this subject (see Jeremiah 33:15-22; Zechariah 14:16-21).

Why Sacrifices?

Why will sacrifices be offered in this temple? Christ's once-for-all sacrifice has taken away sin and has caused the Mosaic law of sacrifices to be abolished (see Hebrews 7–10). Why, then, is the sacrificial system predicted here? John F. Walvoord summarizes the question this way:

> The question is naturally raised why the sacrifices would be observed in the millennium if the sacrifice of Christ once for all fulfilled the typical expectation of the Old Testament sacrificial system. While other objections are also made of a lesser character, it is obvious that this constitutes the major obstacle, not only to accepting the sacrificial system but the possibility of the future temple in the millennium as well.[2]

In answering this issue, we begin with the observation that Israel and the church are not only distinct today (1 Corinthians 10:32; Romans 9–11) but will also be distinct in the millennial kingdom. We might surmise, then, that temple activities in the millennium relate primarily to Israel (though redeemed Gentiles can also participate) and not to the church (see Isaiah 60–61).

This being the case, some Bible expositors have surmised that the millennial sacrifices will be a kind of Jewish memorial of the awful price Christ—the Lamb of God, who now lives in their midst—had to pay for the salvation of these believing but not yet glorified Jews. (They are yet in their mortal bodies, having entered into the millennial kingdom following the tribulation, which they survived.) The temple system will thus allegedly function much like the Lord's Supper does today, as a memorial ritual (1 Corinthians 11:25-26; see also Isaiah 56:7; 66:20-23; Jeremiah 33:17-18; Ezekiel 43:18-27; 45:13–46:24; Malachi 3:3-4).

> According to this view the sacrifices offered during the earthly reign of Christ will be visible reminders of His work on the cross. Thus, these sacrifices will not have any efficacy except to memorialize Christ's death. The primary support for this argument is the parallel of the Lord's Supper. It is argued that just as the communion table looks back on the Cross without besmirching its glory, so millennial sacrifices will do the same.[3]

The problem with this viewpoint is that Ezekiel says the sacrifices are "to make atonement" (Ezekiel 45:15,17,20). The "memorial" viewpoint seems to fall short of explaining these sacrifices.

The solution may be that the purpose of the sacrifices in the millennial temple is to remove ceremonial uncleanness and prevent defilement from polluting the purity of the temple environment. According to this view, such will be necessary because Yahweh will again be dwelling on the earth in the midst of sinful (and therefore unclean) mortal people. (Remember, these people survive the tribulation period and enter the millennial kingdom in their mortal bodies. They retain their sin natures even though they are redeemed by Christ as believers.) The sacrifices will thus remove any ceremonial uncleanness in the temple.

> Because of God's promise to dwell on earth during the millennium (as stated in the New Covenant), it is necessary

that He protect His presence through sacrifice…It should further be added that this sacrificial system will be a temporary one in that the millennium (with its partial population of unglorified humanity) will last only one thousand years. During the eternal state all inhabitants of the New Jerusalem will be glorified and will therefore not be a source of contagious impurities to defile the holiness of Yahweh.[4]

Seen in this light, the sacrifices are not a return to the Mosaic law. The law has forever been done away with through Jesus Christ (Romans 6:14-15; 7:1-6; 1 Corinthians 9:20-21; 2 Corinthians 3:7-11; Galatians 4:1-7; 5:18; Hebrews 8:13; 10:1-14). The sacrifices relate only to removing ritual impurities in the temple as long as fallen but redeemed human beings remain on earth.

Christ Reigns from the Davidic Throne

God promised David that one of his descendants would rule forever on his throne (2 Samuel 7:12-13; 22:51). Like the land promise to Abraham and his descendants, this is an unconditional covenant. It did not depend on David in any way for its fulfillment. David realized this when he received the promise from God, and he responded with humility and a recognition of God's sovereignty over human affairs.

The three key words of the covenant are *kingdom*, *house*, and *throne*. Such words point to the political future of Israel. The word translated *house* here refers to a royal dynasty.

This covenant finds its ultimate fulfillment in Jesus Christ, who was born from the line of David (Matthew 1:1). In the millennial kingdom, He will rule from the throne of David in Jerusalem (Micah 4:1-5; Zephaniah 3:14-20; Zechariah 14). This reign of Christ during the millennial kingdom will extend beyond the Jews to include the Gentile nations as well. Multiple prophecies in Scripture point to Christ's reign during the millennial kingdom:

- "May he have dominion from sea to sea, and from the River to the ends of the earth!" (Psalm 72:8).

- "For to us a child is born, to us a son is given; and the

government shall be upon his shoulder, and his name shall
be called Wonderful Counselor, Mighty God, Everlasting Father, Prince of Peace. Of the increase of his government and of peace there will be no end, on the throne of
David and over his kingdom, to establish it and to uphold
it with justice and with righteousness from this time forth
and forevermore. The zeal of the LORD of hosts will do this"
(Isaiah 9:6-7).

- "I saw in the night visions, and behold, with the clouds of
  heaven there came one like a son of man, and he came to
  the Ancient of Days and was presented before him. And to
  him was given dominion and glory and a kingdom, that
  all peoples, nations, and languages should serve him; his
  dominion is an everlasting dominion, which shall not pass
  away, and his kingdom one that shall not be destroyed"
  (Daniel 7:13-14).

- "He shall speak peace to the nations; his rule shall be from
  sea to sea, and from the River to the ends of the earth"
  (Zechariah 9:10; see also Revelation 20:4).

Note also that when the angel Gabriel appeared to the young virgin Mary to inform her that the Messiah was to be born through her
womb, he spoke to her in Davidic terms.

And the angel said to her, "Do not be afraid, Mary, for you
have found favor with God. And behold, you will conceive in your womb and bear a son, and you shall call his
name Jesus. He will be great and will be called the Son of
the Most High. And the Lord God will give to him the
throne of his father David, and he will reign over the house
of Jacob forever, and of his kingdom there will be no end"
(Luke 1:30-33).

The three key words used by the angel to describe the future rule
of Jesus Christ were *throne*, *house*, and *kingdom*—the same words God

used when He promised David that one from his line would rule forever (2 Samuel 7:16).

Gabriel's words must have immediately brought these Old Testament promises to mind for Mary, a devout young Jew. Indeed, Gabriel's words constituted a clear announcement that Mary's Son would come into this world to fulfill the promise given to David that one of his sons would sit on his throne and rule over his kingdom.

Now that the millennial kingdom is instituted following the second coming of Jesus the Messiah, these long-anticipated prophetic promises are fulfilled: Christ reigns from the throne of David.

Resurrected Saints Reign with Christ

Scripture promises that Christ will gloriously reign from the Davidic throne. But Scripture also promises that the saints will reign with Christ. In 2 Timothy 2:12, for example, the apostle Paul instructs, "If we endure, we will also reign with him." Those who endure through trials will one day rule with Christ in His future kingdom.

This provides an interesting parallel between Jesus Christ and Christians. Christ Himself endured and will one day reign (1 Corinthians 15:25). In the same way—though obviously to a much lesser degree, and under the lordship of Christ—believers must endure and will one day reign with Him (Revelation 3:21).

The idea of reigning with Christ is compatible with what we learn elsewhere in the book of Revelation. For example, Revelation 5:10 reveals that believers have been made "a kingdom and priests to our God, and they shall reign on the earth." Revelation 20:6 makes a similar affirmation: "Blessed and holy is the one who shares in the first resurrection! Over such the second death has no power, but they will be priests of God and of Christ, and they will reign with him for a thousand years."

Even beyond the millennial kingdom and into the eternal state, this privilege of reigning with Christ continues. "Night will be no more. They will need no light of lamp or sun, for the Lord God will be their light, and they will reign forever and ever" (Revelation 22:5). What an awesome privilege and blessing!

In what capacity will believers reign? People's rank or office, as it were, will apparently be commensurate with their commitment and faithfulness during their earthly lives. How wonderful it would be to hear these words from Christ: "Well done, good and faithful servant. You have been faithful over a little; I will set you over much" (Matthew 25:21).

Christ Brings Physical Blessings

Scripture reveals that those who enter into Christ's millennial kingdom will enjoy some unique physical blessings. These six are representative sampling.

1. People will live in a blessed and enhanced environment.

> The wilderness and the dry land shall be glad; the desert shall rejoice and blossom like the crocus; it shall blossom abundantly and rejoice with joy and singing. The glory of Lebanon shall be given to it, the majesty of Carmel and Sharon. They shall see the glory of the LORD, the majesty of our God (Isaiah 35:1-2).

2. Rain and food will be plentiful.

> And he will give rain for the seed with which you sow the ground, and bread, the produce of the ground, which will be rich and plenteous. In that day your livestock will graze in large pastures, and the oxen and the donkeys that work the ground will eat seasoned fodder, which has been winnowed with shovel and fork (Isaiah 30:23-24).

3. Animals will live in harmony with each other and with humans.

> The wolf shall dwell with the lamb, and the leopard shall lie down with the young goat, and the calf and the lion and the fattened calf together; and a little child shall lead them. The cow and the bear shall graze; their young shall lie down together; and the lion shall eat straw like the ox (Isaiah 11:6-7).

4. Longevity will be greatly increased.

> No more shall there be in it an infant who lives but a few days, or an old man who does not fill out his days, for the young man shall die a hundred years old, and the sinner a hundred years old shall be accursed (Isaiah 65:20).

5. Physical infirmities and illnesses will be removed.

> In that day the deaf shall hear the words of a book, and out of their gloom and darkness the eyes of the blind shall see (Isaiah 29:18).

> And no inhabitant will say, "I am sick"; the people who dwell there will be forgiven their iniquity (Isaiah 33:24).

6. Prosperity will prevail, resulting in joy and gladness.

> They shall come and sing aloud on the height of Zion, and they shall be radiant over the goodness of the LORD, over the grain, the wine, and the oil, and over the young of the flock and the herd; their life shall be like a watered garden, and they shall languish no more. Then shall the young women rejoice in the dance, and the young men and the old shall be merry. I will turn their mourning into joy; I will comfort them, and give them gladness for sorrow. I will feast the soul of the priests with abundance, and my people shall be satisfied with my goodness, declares the LORD (Jeremiah 31:12-14).

These and many other physical blessings will be abundantly present during the future millennial kingdom.

Christ Institutes a Perfect Government

Scripture reveals that Christ will institute a perfect government in the millennial kingdom. Here are five representative characteristics of His government.

1. Christ's government will be global.

"As for me, I have set my King on Zion, my holy hill." I will tell of the decree: The LORD said to me, "You are my Son; today I have begotten you. Ask of me, and I will make the nations your heritage, and the ends of the earth your possession. You shall break them with a rod of iron and dash them in pieces like a potter's vessel" (Psalm 2:6-9).

And to him was given dominion and glory and a kingdom, that all peoples, nations, and languages should serve him; his dominion is an everlasting dominion, which shall not pass away, and his kingdom one that shall not be destroyed (Daniel 7:14).

2. Christ's global government will be centered in Jerusalem.

It shall come to pass in the latter days that the mountain of the house of the LORD shall be established as the highest of the mountains, and shall be lifted up above the hills; and all the nations shall flow to it, and many peoples shall come, and say: "Come, let us go up to the mountain of the LORD, to the house of the God of Jacob, that he may teach us his ways and that we may walk in his paths." For out of Zion shall go the law, and the word of the LORD from Jerusalem. He shall judge between the nations (Isaiah 2:2-4; see also Jeremiah 3:17; Ezekiel 48:30-35; Joel 3:16-17; Micah 4:1,6-8; Zechariah 8:2-3).

3. Jesus will reign on the throne of David.

Behold, the days are coming, declares the LORD, when I will raise up for David a righteous Branch, and he shall reign as king and deal wisely, and shall execute justice and righteousness in the land. In his days Judah will be saved, and Israel will dwell securely. And this is the name by which he will be called: "The LORD is our righteousness" (Jeremiah 23:5-6).

4. Christ's government will be perfect and effective.

> For to us a child is born, to us a son is given; and the government shall be upon his shoulder, and his name shall be called Wonderful Counselor, Mighty God, Everlasting Father, Prince of Peace. Of the increase of his government and of peace there will be no end, on the throne of David and over his kingdom, to establish it and to uphold it with justice and with righteousness from this time forth and forevermore. The zeal of the LORD of hosts will do this (Isaiah 9:6-7).

5. Christ's government will bring lasting global peace.

> He shall judge between many peoples, and shall decide for strong nations afar off; and they shall beat their swords into plowshares, and their spears into pruning hooks; nation shall not lift up sword against nation, neither shall they learn war anymore; but they shall sit every man under his vine and under his fig tree, and no one shall make them afraid, for the mouth of the LORD of hosts has spoken (Micah 4:3-4).

In short, Christ's government will yield an ideal climate for living on earth. Christ will succeed where all human governments have failed!

Christ Bestows Great Spiritual Blessing

Christ will bring great spiritual blessing in His millennial kingdom. These blessings relate to the wonderful reality that Jesus Christ Himself will be present with His people on earth. Christ being with His people on earth will affect "the spiritual life of the human race to an extent never realized in previous dispensations."[5]

No wonder Isaiah the prophet tells us that "the earth shall be full of the knowledge of the LORD as the waters cover the sea" (Isaiah 11:9). When we combine this fact with the reality that Satan will be bound during the millennial kingdom (Revelation 20:1-3), we can scarcely imagine the depth of spiritual blessings that will prevail on earth during this time.

The spiritual blessings that will predominate during the millennial kingdom are based on the new covenant (Jeremiah 31:31-34). As an outworking of this wondrous covenant, abundant spiritual blessings will shower the earth. Here are seven examples.

1. The Holy Spirit will be present and will indwell all believers.

> I will pour my Spirit upon your offspring, and my blessing on your descendants (Isaiah 44:3).

> I will put my Spirit within you, and cause you to walk in my statutes and be careful to obey my rules (Ezekiel 36:27).

> And I will put my Spirit within you, and you shall live, and I will place you in your own land. Then you shall know that I am the LORD; I have spoken, and I will do it, declares the LORD (Ezekiel 37:14).

> And it shall come to pass afterward, that I will pour out my Spirit on all flesh; your sons and your daughters shall prophesy, your old men shall dream dreams, and your young men shall see visions. Even on the male and female servants in those days I will pour out my Spirit (Joel 2:28-29).

2. Righteousness will prevail around the world.

> I bring near my righteousness; it is not far off, and my salvation will not delay; I will put salvation in Zion, for Israel my glory (Isaiah 46:13).

> My righteousness draws near, my salvation has gone out, and my arms will judge the peoples; the coastlands hope for me, and for my arm they wait (Isaiah 51:5).

> Your people shall all be righteous; they shall possess the land forever, the branch of my planting, the work of my hands, that I might be glorified (Isaiah 60:21).

3. Obedience to the Lord will prevail.

> All the ends of the earth shall remember and turn to the LORD, and all the families of the nations shall worship before you (Psalm 22:27).

> This is the covenant that I will make with the house of Israel after those days, declares the LORD: I will put my law within them, and I will write it on their hearts. And I will be their God, and they shall be my people (Jeremiah 31:33).

4. Holiness will prevail.

> And a highway shall be there, and it shall be called the Way of Holiness; the unclean shall not pass over it. It shall belong to those who walk on the way…The ransomed of the LORD shall return and come to Zion with singing; everlasting joy shall be upon their heads; they shall obtain gladness and joy, and sorrow and sighing shall flee away (Isaiah 35:8-10).

> You shall know that I am the LORD your God, who dwells in Zion, my holy mountain. And Jerusalem shall be holy, and strangers shall never again pass through it (Joel 3:17).

5. Faithfulness will prevail.

> Steadfast love and faithfulness meet; righteousness and peace kiss each other. Faithfulness springs up from the ground, and righteousness looks down from the sky (Psalm 85:10-11).

> Thus says the LORD: I have returned to Zion and will dwell in the midst of Jerusalem, and Jerusalem shall be called the faithful city, and the mountain of the LORD of hosts, the holy mountain (Zechariah 8:3).

6. All the world's residents will worship the Messiah.

From the rising of the sun to its setting my name will be great among the nations, and in every place incense will be offered to my name, and a pure offering. For my name will be great among the nations, says the LORD of hosts (Malachi 1:11).

At that time I will change the speech of the peoples to a pure speech, that all of them may call upon the name of the LORD and serve him with one accord (Zephaniah 3:9).

Thus says the LORD of hosts: In those days ten men from the nations of every tongue shall take hold of the robe of a Jew, saying, "Let us go with you, for we have heard that God is with you" (Zechariah 8:23).

7. God's presence will be made manifest.

My dwelling place shall be with them, and I will be their God, and they shall be my people. Then the nations will know that I am the LORD who sanctifies Israel, when my sanctuary is in their midst forevermore (Ezekiel 37:27-28).

Sing and rejoice, O daughter of Zion, for behold, I come and I will dwell in your midst, declares the LORD. And many nations shall join themselves to the LORD in that day, and shall be my people. And I will dwell in your midst, and you shall know that the LORD of hosts has sent me to you (Zechariah 2:10-13).

How awesome it will all be!

After the Millennial Kingdom

IN THIS CHAPTER

Satan Leads a Final Revolt

The bottomless pit presently serves as the place of imprisonment of some demonic spirits (Luke 8:31; 2 Peter 2:4). The devil and all demonic spirits will be bound here for 1000 years during Christ's millennial kingdom (Revelation 20:1-3). This quarantine will effectively remove a powerfully destructive and deceptive force in all areas of human life and thought during Christ's kingdom.

Revelation 20:7-8 warns, however, that "when the thousand years are ended, Satan will be released from his prison and will come out to deceive the nations that are at the four corners of the earth, Gog and Magog, to gather them for battle; their number is like the sand of the sea." He will move his forces against Jerusalem with fervor.

Of course, deception has always been at the very heart of Satan's activities. "He was a murderer from the beginning, and has nothing to do with the truth, because there is no truth in him. When he lies, he speaks out of his own character, for he is a liar and the father of lies" (John 8:44). So when he engages in deception, he is in character. Recall that he used a lie to bring spiritual and physical death to humankind (see Genesis 3:4,13; 1 John 3:8,10-15).

Who Will Join Sides with Satan?

Even though the millennium will involve the perfect government of Christ, it will also include mortal and fallen human beings. To be sure, Matthew 25:31-46 is clear that only believers are invited into Christ's millennial kingdom. But these people will give birth to babies and raise children, some of whom will not necessarily choose to follow Jesus Christ. As long as they do not externally rebel against the government of Christ, they are permitted to live during the millennial kingdom. But all outward rebellion will be stopped instantly.

When Satan is released at the end of the millennium, he will lead many of these unbelievers astray in a massive rebellion against Christ. As the text says, "their number is like the sand of the sea" (Revelation 20:8). This will represent Satan's last stand.

The Attack Against Jerusalem Nullified

Jerusalem, the headquarters of Christ's government throughout the millennial kingdom (Isaiah 2:1-5), will be the target city of the satanic revolt. Fire instantly comes down upon the invaders (Revelation 20:9), a common mode of God's judgment (see Genesis 19:24; Exodus 9:23-24; Leviticus 9:24; 10:2; Numbers 11:1; 16:35; 26:10; 1 Kings 18:38; 2 Kings 1:10,12,14; 1 Chronicles 21:26; 2 Chronicles 7:1,3; Psalm 11:6). The rebellion is squashed instantly; it had no chance of success.

A Clarification on Gog and Magog

Earlier in the book I noted that the Ezekiel invasion against Israel (by Russia, Iran, Sudan, Turkey, and a number of other Muslim nations) will likely take place prior to the tribulation period (Ezekiel 38–39). Some interpreters, however, believe this invasion must take place after the millennial kingdom because Revelation 20:7-8 mentions Gog and Magog.

In both cases, a large number of soldiers are mentioned. In the Ezekiel invasion, we read that "many peoples are with you" (Ezekiel 38:6,15). Likewise, the invasion force mentioned in Revelation is massive, for "their number is like the sand of the sea" (Revelation 20:8). As well, in both cases, God is the one who defeats the invaders (Ezekiel 39:3-6; Revelation 20:9).

But this view is problematic on several levels. Foundationally, the chronology is all wrong. The invasion described in Ezekiel 38–39 is part of a larger section of Ezekiel's book that deals with the restoration of Israel (chapters 33–39). This is followed by another large section of Ezekiel's book that describes the Jewish millennial temple and the restoration of sacrifices (chapters 40–48). In other words, Ezekiel's invasion is before the millennial kingdom. By contrast, the invasion described in Revelation 20:7-10 takes place after the millennial kingdom, so these invasions are separated by a thousand years.

The seven months required to bury dead bodies (following the Ezekiel invasion) doesn't make sense in a scenario at the end of the millennial kingdom. Think about it. In Ezekiel's scenario, the Israelites spend seven hard months burying the wicked dead who invaded them. In the Revelation scenario, the wicked dead are resurrected in order to take part in the great white throne judgment and be thrown into the lake of fire. Besides, Revelation 20:9 tells us that "fire came down from heaven and consumed them." There won't be any bodies left to bury because they'll all be incinerated.

Further, the next events in the book of Revelation are the great white throne judgment and the beginning of the eternal state (Revelation 21). This naturally brings up the problem of the burning of weapons for seven years. If this invasion takes place at the end of the millennial kingdom, then the burning of weapons would have to go beyond the millennial kingdom and into the eternal state, which doesn't make any sense at all.

We can also observe that in the Ezekiel invasion, a coalition of localized nations (Russia and a number of Muslim nations) invade from the north. The invasion at the end of the millennium is by a broader coalition—"nations that are at the four corners of the earth" (Revelation 20:8).

Still further, the invasion prophesied by Ezekiel occurs relatively soon after Israel's rebirth as a nation and the ingathering of Jewish people from around the world (Ezekiel 36–37). The invasion mentioned in Revelation 20:7-10, by contrast, occurs after Jesus has been reigning on earth for a thousand years.

As well, in Ezekiel the invasion will be the catalyst God will use to draw Israel to Himself (see Ezekiel 39:7,22-29) and to put an end to its captivity. The battle in Revelation 20, however, will occur after Israel has been faithful to her God and has enjoyed His blessings for 1000 years.

But if these are two separate invasions, why did the apostle John use the terms Gog and Magog to describe the postmillennial satanic invasion against Jerusalem? It seems likely that John was simply using the terms Gog and Magog as a shorthand metaphor, much as we do today. For example, the term Wall Street has come to metaphorically refer to the stock market. Likewise, in New Testament times, terms like Corinthian and Nazarene came to metaphorically refer to people with less than desirable qualities. Whether among modern people or people in New Testament times, the meanings of these words are clear to the hearers.

Likewise, when John used the terms Gog and Magog in Revelation 20:7-10, his readers no doubt immediately drew the right connection and understood that this invasion at the end of the millennium would be similar to what Ezekiel described. A confederation of nations will attack Israel but not succeed. In other words, this was to be a Gog-and-Magog-like invasion.

Satan Is Cast into the Lake of Fire

Revelation 20:10 tells us that following the final revolt against Christ, "the devil who had deceived [the saints] was thrown into the lake of fire and sulfur where the beast and the false prophet were, and they will be tormented day and night forever and ever." Notice that all three persons of the satanic trinity—Satan, the antichrist, and the false prophet—will suffer the same dire destiny. More specifically, the antichrist and the false prophet will be thrown into the lake of fire prior to the beginning of the millennial kingdom. They will have been burning there for 1000 years when Satan joins them, and all three will continue to burn for all eternity. They will receive their just due.

Notice also that Satan is not the only fallen angel who will be judged and confined to the lake of fire. All demons who have served under him will also be judged. Matthew 25:41 refers to "the eternal fire prepared for the devil and his angels" (see also 2 Peter 2:4; Jude 6). The demonic spirits who have been harassing Christians throughout the ages will one day receive a just judgment!

The Second Resurrection

Scripture is clear that those who will participate in the great white throne judgment—that is, the wicked dead—will be resurrected to judgment. Jesus Himself affirmed that "a time is coming when all who are in their graves will hear his voice and come out—those who have done good will rise to live, and those who have done evil will rise to be condemned" (John 5:28-29 NIV).

To clarify, Jesus is not teaching that there is just one general resurrection that will take place at the end of time. Contrary to this idea, the Scriptures refer to two resurrections (Revelation 20:5-6,11-15). The first resurrection is the resurrection of the saved, and the second resurrection is the resurrection of the wicked (unsaved).

We can be even more specific. The term *first resurrection* refers to all the resurrections of the righteous, even though they are widely separated in time. One resurrection of the righteous occurs at the rapture, before the tribulation period (1 Thessalonians 4:16); another at the end of the tribulation period (Revelation 20:4); and still another at the end of the 1000-year millennial kingdom. They all are "first" in the sense of being before the second (final) resurrection of the wicked. Accordingly, the term *first resurrection* applies to all the resurrections of the saints regardless of when they occur, including the resurrection of Christ Himself.

This is a wondrous resurrection, for God's people will now have bodies in which the perishable has become imperishable, and the mortal has become immortal. These bodies will be specially designed to enable us to live directly in the presence of God for all eternity, never getting sick and never dying.

The second resurrection, by contrast, is an awful spectacle. All the unsaved of all time will be resurrected at the end of Christ's millennial kingdom and be judged at the great white throne judgment (Revelation 20:11-15).

The bodies of the unsaved will also be imperishable and immortal. Their bodies will be eternal bodies, and though they will suffer the fires of hell, they will not burn up, but will last for all eternity in an environment of suffering. How horrific are the eternal consequences for choosing against Christ.

The Wicked Dead Are Judged

Unlike believers, whose judgment deals only with rewards and loss of rewards, unbelievers face a horrific judgment that leads to their being cast into the lake of fire. As we have seen, this is the great white throne judgment (Revelation 20:11-15). Christ Himself will judge the unsaved dead of all time. This judgment takes place after the millennial kingdom, Christ's 1000-year reign on the earth.

We know that this judgment takes place after the millennial kingdom, for Revelation 20, after describing the millennium, states: "*Then* I saw a great white throne and him who was seated on it" (verse 11). In other words, the millennium first takes place, and the judgment follows.

Those who face Christ at this judgment will be judged on the basis of their works (verses 12-13). It is critical to understand that they actually appear at this judgment because they are already unsaved. This judgment will not separate believers from unbelievers, for all who will experience it will have already made the choice during their lifetimes to reject God. Once they are before the divine Judge, they are judged according to their works not only to justify their condemnation but also to determine the degree to which each person should be punished throughout eternity.

When Christ opens the book of life, no name of anyone present at the great white throne judgment is in it. Their names do not appear in the book of life because they have rejected the source of life—Jesus Christ. Because they rejected the source of life, they are cast into the lake of fire, which constitutes the second death (verse 14) and involves eternal separation from God.

All those who are judged at the great white throne judgment have a horrible destiny ahead that includes weeping and gnashing of teeth (Matthew 13:41-42), condemnation (Matthew 12:36-37), destruction (Philippians 1:28), eternal punishment (Matthew 25:46), separation from God's presence (2 Thessalonians 1:8-9), and trouble and distress (Romans 2:9).

Nevertheless, the Scriptures also indicate that there will be degrees of punishment in hell (Matthew 10:15; 16:27; Luke 12:47-48; Revelation 20:12-13; 22:12). These degrees of punishment will be determined at the great white throne judgment when Christ examines each person with His penetrating eyes.

Common observation shows that unsaved people vary as much in their quality of life as saved people do. For example, some saved people are spiritual and charitable, and other saved people are carnal and unloving. Some unbelievers are terribly evil (like Hitler), while others—such as unbelieving moralists—are much less evil.

Just as believers have varied responses to God's law and will have corresponding rewards in heaven, so unbelievers have various responses to God's law and therefore will have corresponding experiences in their punishment in hell. Just as there are degrees of reward in heaven, so there are degrees of punishment in hell. The great white throne judgment will apportion perfectly fair judgments against the wicked dead.

The Lake of Fire

The lake of fire will be the eternal abode of Satan, demons, the antichrist, the false prophet, and unbelievers throughout all history (Revelation 19:20; 20:10-15). It will be populated by unsaved human beings following the great white throne judgment. All residents will be tormented day and night forever and ever. It is eternal.

The lake of fire is another term for hell. The Scriptures assure us that hell is a real place. But hell was not part of God's original creation, which He called good (Genesis 1). Hell was created later to accommodate the banishment of Satan and his fallen angels who rebelled against God (Matthew 25:41). Human beings who reject Christ will join Satan and his fallen angels in this infernal place of suffering.

Scripture describes the destiny of the wicked as a fiery furnace. Jesus said that in this fiery furnace would be weeping and gnashing of teeth (Matthew 13:42). This weeping will be caused by the environment, the company, the remorse and guilt, and the shame that afflicts all who are in hell.

Scripture uses a number of other terms to describe the horrors of hell, including unquenchable fire (Mark 9:47-48), the fiery lake of burning sulfur (Revelation 19:20), eternal fire (Matthew 18:8), eternal punishment (Matthew 25:46), destruction (Matthew 7:13), everlasting destruction (2 Thessalonians 1:8-9), the place of weeping and gnashing of teeth (Matthew 13:42), and the second death (Revelation 20:14). The horror of hell is inconceivable to the human mind.

What precisely is the fire of hell (or lake of fire)? Some believe it is literal. Indeed, that may very well be the case. Others believe fire is a metaphor for the great wrath of God. Scripture commonly uses this image.

- "The LORD your God is a consuming fire, a jealous God" (Deuteronomy 4:24).

- "God is a consuming fire" (Hebrews 12:29).

- "His wrath is poured out like fire" (Nahum 1:6).

- "Who can stand when he appears? For he will be like a refiner's fire" (Malachi 3:2).

- God said, "My wrath will flare up and burn like fire because of the evil you have done—burn with no one to quench it" (Jeremiah 4:4 NIV).

How awful is the fiery wrath of God!

The best English translations of the Old Testament don't include the word *hell*. Instead, they transliterate the Hebrew word *Sheol*. *Sheol* can have different meanings in different contexts. Sometimes the word means "grave." Other times it refers to the place of departed people in contrast to the state of living people. The Old Testament portrays Sheol as a place of horror (Psalm 55:15) and punishment (Job 24:19; Psalm 9:17).

When we get to the New Testament, we find that a number of words relate to the doctrine of hell. Hades seems to be the New Testament counterpart to Sheol. The rich man endured great suffering in Hades (Luke 16:23).

However, this was an intermediate state and not the rich man's eternal destiny. Hades is a temporary abode and will one day be cast into the lake of fire. In the future, the wicked in Hades will be raised from the dead and judged at the great white throne judgment. They will then be cast into the lake of fire, which will be their permanent place of suffering throughout all eternity.

Another word related to the concept of hell is *Gehenna* (Matthew 10:28). This word has an interesting history. For several generations, ancient Israel committed atrocities in the Valley of Ben Hinnom—including human sacrifices, and even the sacrifice of children (2 Kings 23:10; 2 Chronicles 28:3; 33:6; Jeremiah 32:35). The unfortunate victims were sacrificed to the false Moabite god Molech. Jeremiah appropriately called this valley a "valley of slaughter" (Jeremiah 7:31-34).

Eventually the valley came to be used as a public rubbish dump into which all the filth in Jerusalem was poured. Not only garbage but also the bodies of dead animals and the corpses of criminals were thrown on the heap, where they perpetually burned. The valley fires never stopped burning. And there was always a good meal for a hungry worm.

This place was originally called (in the Hebrew) *Ge[gen]hinnom* (the valley of the son[s] of Hinnom). It was eventually shortened to the name *Ge-Hinnom*. The Greek translation of this Hebrew phrase is *Gehenna*. It became an appropriate and graphic term for the reality of hell. Jesus Himself used the word 11 times in reference to the eternal place of suffering of unredeemed humanity.

The Eternal State

Christ Delivers the Kingdom to the Father

Many people have struggled to understand 1 Corinthians 15:24,28, where Paul says of Jesus Christ, "Then comes the end, when he delivers the kingdom to God the Father...When all things are subjected to him, then the Son himself will also be subjected to him who put all things in subjection under him, that God may be all in all."

It is important to grasp the meaning of these verses. Notice that even though Jesus Christ is completely equal to the Father in terms of being God (see, for example, John 1:1; 8:58; 10:30; Philippians 2:5-11; Colossians 2:9), Christ is nevertheless in subjection to the Father (John 14:28; 1 Corinthians 11:3). Many theologians point out that Jesus not only is God but also took upon Himself a human nature in the incarnation—a human nature He still possesses today (see Luke 24:37-39; Acts 2:31; 1 Timothy 2:5; 1 John 4:2; 2 John 7).

Because Christ still possesses His human nature, He is still in submission to the Father. Even apart from His humanity, however, Jesus has always been and forever will be in subjection to the Father because this is the nature of the relationship of the persons in the Trinity.

This is one of the theological factors behind such verses as John 3:17: "God did not send his Son into the world to condemn the world, but in order that the world might be saved through him." God the Father is the sender; Jesus is the sent one.

What, then, is the meaning of 1 Corinthians 15:28? In the eternal plan of salvation, the eternal Son's role was to become the Mediator (the go-between) between man and God the Father. In 1 Timothy 2:5, for example, we read, "There is one God, and there is one mediator between God and men, the man Christ Jesus."

It is important to recognize, however, that Christ's role as mediator is a temporary one. This role is not eternal. When the task of human redemption is finally complete, Christ the mediator voluntarily surrenders the kingdom to the one who sent Him into the world to accomplish redemption, God the Father.

At that time, the Son's role as mediator will be completed. As one Bible expositor put it, "When he delivers up the administration of the earthly kingdom to the Father, then the triune God will reign as God and no longer through the incarnate Son."[1] Indeed, "throughout the endless ages of eternity, the triune God Jehovah will permeate the universe with His celestial love and glory. God will then be immediately known by all. What a glorious destiny awaits the redeemed of the Lord."[2]

The Old Heavens and Earth Are Destroyed

As we think back to the scene in the Garden of Eden in which Adam and Eve sinned against God, we remember that God judged the earth with a curse (Genesis 3:17-18). Indeed, the universe was subjected to futility and is now in bondage to decay (Romans 8:20-22).

So before the eternal kingdom can be made manifest, God must deal with this cursed earth and universe. And Satan has long carried out his evil schemes on earth (see Ephesians 2:2), so the earth must be purged of all stains resulting from his extended presence.

In short, the earth, along with the first and second heavens—that is, the earth's atmosphere (Job 35:5) and the stellar universe (Genesis 1:17; Deuteronomy 17:3)—must be renewed. The old must make room for the new.

The Scriptures often speak of the passing of the old heavens and earth. Psalm 102:25-26 is an example: "Of old you [O God] laid the foundation of the earth, and the heavens are the work of your hands. They will perish, but you will remain; they will all wear out like a garment. You will change them like a robe, and they will pass away." Isaiah 51:6 is another: "Lift up your eyes to the heavens, and look at the earth beneath; for the heavens vanish like smoke, the earth will wear out like a garment...but my salvation will be forever." This reminds us of Jesus' words in Matthew 24:35: "Heaven and earth will pass away, but my words will not pass away."

Perhaps the most extended section of Scripture dealing with the passing of the old heavens and earth is 2 Peter 3:7-13.

> The heavens and earth that now exist are stored up for fire, being kept until the day of judgment and destruction of the ungodly.
>
> But do not overlook this one fact, beloved, that with the Lord one day is as a thousand years, and a thousand years as one day. The Lord is not slow to fulfill his promise as some count slowness, but is patient toward you, not wishing that any should perish, but that all should reach repentance. But the day of the Lord will come like a thief, and then the heavens will pass away with a roar, and the heavenly bodies will be burned up and dissolved, and the earth and the works that are done on it will be exposed.
>
> Since all these things are thus to be dissolved, what sort of people ought you to be in lives of holiness and godliness, waiting for and hastening the coming of the day of God, because of which the heavens will be set on fire and dissolved, and the heavenly bodies will melt as they burn! But

according to his promise we are waiting for new heavens
and a new earth in which righteousness dwells.

The old must pass to make room for the new. That which is stained
and decaying must make room for that which will be utterly pure and
eternal.

The New Heaven and New Earth

After the universe is cleansed by fire and God creates a new heaven
and a new earth, all vestiges of the curse and Satan's presence will be
utterly and forever removed from all creation. Bible expositor Albert
Barnes makes this comment:

> The earth will be no more cursed, and will produce no
> more thorns and thistles; man will be no more compelled
> to earn his bread by the sweat of his brow; woman will be
> no more doomed to bear the sufferings which she does
> now; and the abodes of the blessed will be no more cursed
> by sickness, sorrow, tears, and death.[3]

All things will be made new, and how blessed it will be!

An Expanded Heaven

Theologians and Bible expositors have been careful to distinguish
between the present heaven where God now dwells and where believers go at the moment of death (2 Corinthians 5:8; Philippians 1:21-23)
and the future heaven where believers will spend all eternity (2 Peter
3:13; Revelation 21:1). For indeed, a renovation is coming.

> In the consummation of all things, God will renovate the
> heavens and the earth, merging His heaven with a new uni-
> verse for a perfect dwelling-place that will be our home for-
> ever. In other words, heaven, the realm where God dwells,
> will expand to encompass the entire universe of creation,
> which will be fashioned into a perfect and glorious domain
> fit for the glory of heaven.[4]

Peter speaks of this glorious future reality in 2 Peter 3:13. You and I can look forward to living eternally in a magnificent kingdom where heaven and earth unite in a glory that exceeds the imaginative capabilities of the finite human brain.

Finally the prophecy of Isaiah 65:17 will be fulfilled, where God promises, "Behold, I create new heavens and a new earth, and the former things shall not be remembered or come into mind." Finally the prophecy of Revelation 21:1,5 will be fulfilled: "Then I saw a new heaven and a new earth, for the first heaven and the first earth had passed away, and the sea was no more…And he who was seated on the throne said, 'Behold, I am making all things new.' Also he said, 'Write this down, for these words are trustworthy and true.'"

A Renewed Universe

The new heaven and earth will be this present universe—only it will be purified of all evil, sin, suffering, and death. The Greek word used to designate the newness of the cosmos is not *neos* but *kainos*. *Neos* means "new in time" or "new in origin." But *kainos* means "new in nature" or "new in quality." So the phrase "new heavens and a new earth" refers not to a cosmos that is totally other than the present cosmos. Rather, the new cosmos will stand in continuity with the present cosmos, but it will be utterly renewed and renovated.

Commentator William Hendrickson explains, "It is the same heaven and earth, but gloriously rejuvenated, with no weeds, thorns, or thistles."[5] J. Oswald Sanders makes a similar comment. "The picture is of the universe transformed, perfected, purged of everything that is evil and that exalts itself against God. It is 'new,' not in the sense of being a new creation, but of being new in character—a worthy milieu for the residents of God's redeemed people."[6]

This means that a resurrected people will live in a resurrected universe! Theologian John Piper puts it this way: "What happens to our bodies and what happens to the creation go together. And what happens to our bodies is not annihilation but redemption…Our bodies will be redeemed, restored, made new, not thrown away. And so it is with the heavens and the earth."[7]

Matthew 19:28 (NASB) thus speaks of "the regeneration." The NIV calls it "the renewal of all things." Acts 3:21 (NASB) mentions the "restoration of all things." (See also Isaiah 65:18-25; Ezekiel 28:25-26; 34:25-30.) The new heavens and earth, like our newness in Christ, will be regenerated, glorified, free from the curse of sin, and eternal. Our planet—indeed, the whole universe—will be put in the crucible, altered, changed, and made new, to abide forever.

The new earth, being a renewed and eternal earth, will be adapted to the vast moral and physical changes that the eternal state necessitates. Everything is new in the eternal state. Everything will be according to God's own glorious nature. The new heavens and the new earth will be brought into blessed conformity with all that God is—in a state of fixed bliss and absolute perfection.

Heaven and Earth Merged

One day heaven and earth will no longer be separate realms, as they are now, but will be merged. Believers will thus continue to be in heaven even while they are on the new earth. The new earth will be utterly sinless. It will be bathed and suffused in the light and splendor of God, which will not be obscured by evil of any kind or darkened by evildoers of any description.

The New Jerusalem

The most elaborate description of the heavenly city contained in the Bible is in Revelation 21.

> I saw the holy city, new Jerusalem, coming down out of heaven from God, prepared as a bride adorned for her husband…having the glory of God, its radiance like a most rare jewel, like a jasper, clear as crystal. It had a great, high wall, with twelve gates, and at the gates twelve angels, and on the gates the names of the twelve tribes of the sons of Israel were inscribed—on the east three gates, on the north three gates, on the south three gates, and on the west three gates. And the wall of the city had twelve foundations, and

on them were the twelve names of the twelve apostles of the Lamb…

The wall was built of jasper, while the city was pure gold, clear as glass. The foundations of the wall of the city were adorned with every kind of jewel…And the twelve gates were twelve pearls, each of the gates made of a single pearl, and the street of the city was pure gold, transparent as glass…

And the city has no need of sun or moon to shine on it, for the glory of God gives it light, and its lamp is the Lamb… And its gates will never be shut by day—and there will be no night there.

This description of the New Jerusalem is astounding. We gaze in amazement at such transcendent splendor that the human mind can scarcely take it in. This is a scene of ecstatic joy and fellowship of sinless angels and redeemed glorified human beings. The voice of the Alpha and the Omega, the beginning and the end, utters a climactic declaration: "Behold, I am making all things new" (Revelation 21:5).

The words contained in Revelation 21–22 no doubt represent a human attempt to describe the utterly indescribable.

The overall impression of the city as a gigantic brilliant jewel compared to jasper, clear as crystal, indicates its great beauty. John was trying to describe what he saw and to relate it to what might be familiar to his readers. However, it is evident that his revelation transcends anything that can be experienced.[8]

Millard Erickson agrees and offers these reflections on the glorious splendor of this heavenly city.

Images suggesting immense size or brilliant light depict heaven as a place of unimaginable splendor, greatness, excellence, and beauty…It is likely that while John's vision employs as metaphors those items which we think of as being most valuable and beautiful, the actual splendor of heaven far exceeds anything that we have yet experienced.[9]

George Marsden, author of *Jonathan Edwards: A Life*, points out that Edwards...

> recounted the similes used in Scripture to describe heaven...
> His larger point was that, however wonderful it might be
> to imagine these things, earthly images are not really ade-
> quate...These biblical images, he explained, are "very faint
> shadows" that represent the joys of heaven humans are
> intended to enjoy.[10]

In short, the heavenly city will be far more wondrous than we can possibly imagine.

One thing is certain. The city is designed to reflect and manifest the incredible glory of God. The mention of transparency reveals that the city is strategically designed to transmit the glory of God in the form of light without hindrance. The human imagination is simply incapable of fathoming the immeasurably resplendent glory of God that will be perpetually manifest in the eternal city. This is especially so considering the fact that all manner of precious stones will be built into the eternal city.

Perfect in Every Way

Because you and I are so accustomed to living in a fallen world that has been viciously marred by sin and corruption, we cannot conceive of what life might be like in a heavenly habitat that is without such sin and fallenness. From birth to death, we are confronted with imperfection on every level. But in the eternal city, we will experience nothing but perfection. I love A.T. Pierson's description.

> There shall be no more curse—*perfect restoration*. The
> throne of God and of the Lamb shall be in it—*perfect
> administration*. His servants shall serve him—*perfect sub-
> ordination*. And they shall see his face—*perfect transforma-
> tion*. And his name shall be on their foreheads—*perfect*

identification. And there shall be no night there; and they need no candle, neither light of the sun; for the Lord giveth them light—*perfect illumination*. And they shall reign forever and ever—*perfect exultation*.[11]

A Huge City

The heavenly city measures approximately 1500 miles by 1500 miles by 1500 miles. Though some interpret these big numbers symbolically, allegedly carrying the idea that "saved people are never crowded," I think the dimensions are intended to be interpreted literally. The eternal city is so huge that it would measure approximately the distance from Canada to Mexico, and from the Atlantic Ocean to the Rockies. That is a surface area of 2.25 million square miles. (By comparison, London is only 621 square miles.) Put another way, the ground level area of the city will be 3623 times that of London. If the city has stories, each being 13 feet high, the city would have 660,000 stories. That is huge!

A city that high might seem to present a formidable challenge to city travelers. We must not forget, however, that our resurrection bodies will likely have amazing capabilities. Some expositors believe our new bodies will have the ability to fly and get places fast. That would be very exciting!

Someone calculated that if this structure is cube-shaped, it would allow for 20 billion residents, each having his or her own private 75-acre cube. If each residence were smaller, the city would have room to accommodate one hundred thousand billion people with plenty of room left over for parks, streets, and other things you would see in any normal city.

The eternal city could either be cube-shaped or pyramid-shaped—and there are good Christian scholars on both sides of the debate. Some prefer to consider it shaped as a pyramid, for this would explain how the river of the water of life could flow down its sides (Revelation 22:1-2). Others prefer to consider it shaped as a cube, for the Holy of Holies in Solomon's Temple was cube-shaped (1 Kings 6:20), and a cubical shape of the New Jerusalem might be intended to communicate that this eternal city is like an eternal Holy of Holies.

High Walls and Open Gates

> [The city] had a great, high wall, with twelve gates, and at
> the gates twelve angels, and on the gates the names of the
> twelve tribes of the sons of Israel were inscribed…And the
> wall of the city had twelve foundations, and on them were
> the twelve names of the twelve apostles of the Lamb (Rev-
> elation 21:12,14).

Perhaps the angels are at each of the 12 gates not only as guardians but also in view of their role as ministering spirits to the heirs of salvation (Hebrews 1:14). Perhaps the names of the 12 tribes of Israel are written on the gates to remind us that "salvation is from the Jews" (John 4:22). And perhaps the names of the apostles appear on the foundations to remind us that the church was built upon these men of God (Ephesians 2:20).

What was John's reaction when he saw his own name inscribed on one of the foundations? What a thrill it must have been. It is like an eternal memorial to John's faithfulness—and the faithfulness of the other apostles—in defending the truth of Jesus Christ in an often hostile world.

Notice that "its gates will never be shut by day—and there will be no night there" (Revelation 21:25). In ancient times, city gates were shut at night to guard against invaders. Gates were part of the city's security. Those who live in the eternal city, however, will never have an external threat. Satan, demons, and unbelievers will be in eternal quarantine in hell. God Himself will dwell within the city. Who would dare attack it?

A River, a Tree, and Healing Leaves

"Then the angel showed me the river of the water of life, bright as crystal, flowing from the throne of God and of the Lamb through the middle of the street of the city" (Revelation 22:1). This pure river of life, though real and material, may also be symbolic of the abundance of spiritual life that will characterize those who are living in the eternal city. The stream seems to symbolize the perpetual outflow of spiritual blessing to all the redeemed of all ages, who are now basking in the full glow of eternal life. What spiritual blessedness there will be in the eternal state.

We next read of the tree of life (Revelation 22:2). The last time we read of the tree of life was in Genesis 3, where Adam and Eve sinned in the Garden of Eden. Paradise was lost. Now, in the book of Revelation, paradise is restored, and we again witness the tree of life in the glorious eternal state.

The leaves on the tree are said to be for the healing of nations. But what does this mean? Will there actually be a need for healing, as if somehow things are not perfect in the eternal state? Albert Barnes suggests, "We are not to suppose that there will be sickness, and a healing process in heaven, for that idea is expressly excluded in Revelation 21:4."[12] This verse informs us that "death shall be no more, neither shall there be mourning nor crying nor pain anymore."

The word used for "healing" in this verse is *therapeia*. We derive the English word *therapy* from this word. The word carries the idea of "health-giving." We should interpret this to mean that the leaves of the tree promote the enjoyment of life in the New Jerusalem and are not for correcting ills that do not exist.

No Sun or Moon Needed

"The city has no need of sun or moon to shine on it, for the glory of God gives it light, and its lamp is the Lamb" (Revelation 21:23). This is in keeping with the prophecy in Isaiah 60:19: "The sun shall be no more your light by day, nor for brightness shall the moon give you light; but the LORD will be your everlasting light, and your God will be your glory." Dr. Lehman Strauss's comments on the Lamb's glory are worthy of meditation.

> In that city which Christ has prepared for His own there will be no created light, simply because Christ Himself, who is the uncreated light (John 8:12), will be there...The created lights of God and of men are as darkness when compared with our Blessed Lord. The light He defuses throughout eternity is the unclouded, undimmed glory of

His own Holy presence. In consequence of the fullness of
that light, there shall be no night.[13]

A Holy City

In Revelation 21:1-2 we find heaven described as "the holy city."
This is a fitting description. Indeed, in this city there will be no sin or
unrighteousness of any kind. Only the pure of heart will dwell there.
This does not mean you and I must personally attain moral perfection in order to dwell there. Those of us who believe in Christ have
been given the very righteousness of Christ (see Romans 4:11,22-24).
Because of what Christ accomplished for us at the cross (taking our
sins upon Himself), we have been made holy (Hebrews 10:14). We will
have the privilege of living for all eternity in the holy city.

Contrasting the New Jerusalem with Earth

As we read John's description of the New Jerusalem, we find a whole
series of contrasts with the earth. These contrasts have been wonder-
fully summarized by Bruce Shelley.

> In contrast to the darkness of most ancient cities, John says
> heaven is always lighted. In contrast to rampant disease in
> the ancient world, he says heaven has trees whose leaves
> heal all sorts of sicknesses. In contrast to the parched des-
> erts of the Near East, he pictures heaven with an endless
> river of crystal-clear water. In contrast to a meager existence
> in an arid climate, John says twelve kinds of fruit grow on
> the trees of heaven. In a word, heaven is a wonderful des-
> tiny, free of the shortages and discomforts of this life.[14]

Finally, the purposes of God are fulfilled. God's plan of salvation,
conceived in eternity past, is now brought into full fruition. And how
glorious it will be. One of the great commentators of times past, Wil-
bur Smith, describes it this way:

> All the glorious purposes of God, ordained from the foun-
> dation of the world, have now been attained. The rebellion

of angels and mankind is finally subdued, as the King of kings assumes his rightful sovereignty. Absolute and unchangeable holiness characterizes all within the universal kingdom of God. The redeemed, made so by the blood of the Lamb, are in resurrection and eternal glory. Life is everywhere—and death will never intrude again. The earth and the heavens both are renewed. Light, beauty, holiness, joy, the presence of God, the worship of God, service to Christ, likeness to Christ—all are now abiding realities. The vocabulary of man, made for life here, is incapable of truly and adequately depicting what God has prepared for those that love him.[15]

The eternal city—the New Jerusalem—will be staggeringly, incomprehensibly wonderful, far more so than any human mind could possibly fathom or even begin to imagine. Christians are merely pilgrims en route to the final frontier of the New Jerusalem, just passing through this brief dot of time on earth.

We are wisest when we choose to daily follow the apostle Paul's advice in Colossians 3:1-2: "Seek the things that are above, where Christ is, seated at the right hand of God. Set your minds on things that are above, not on things that are on earth."

To him who loves us
and has freed us from our sins by his blood
and made us a kingdom,
priests to his God and Father,
to him be glory and dominion forever and ever.
Amen.

Revelation 1:5-6

Bibliography

Ankerberg, John, and Dillon Burroughs. *Middle East Meltdown*. Eugene: Harvest House, 2007.

Berkhof, Louis. *Manual of Christian Doctrine*. Grand Rapids: Eerdmans, 1983.

———. *Systematic Theology*. Grand Rapids: Eerdmans, 1977.

Block, Daniel. *The Book of Ezekiel: Chapters 25–48*. Grand Rapids: Eerdmans, 1998.

Buswell, James. *A Systematic Theology of the Christian Religion*. Grand Rapids: Zondervan, 1979.

Demar, Gary. *End Times Fiction*. Nashville: Thomas Nelson, 2001.

Erickson, Millard. *Christian Theology*. Grand Rapids: Baker, 1985.

Feinberg, Charles. *The Prophecy of Ezekiel*. Eugene: Wipf and Stock, 2003.

Fruchtenbaum, Arnold. *The Footsteps of the Messiah*. San Antonio: Ariel, 2004.

Geisler, Norman. *Systematic Theology*. Minneapolis: Bethany House, 2005.

Geisler, Norman, and William Nix. *General Introduction to the Bible*. Chicago: Moody, 1986.

Harrison, Everett, ed. *Baker's Dictionary of Theology*. Grand Rapids: Baker Books, 1960.

Hays, J. Daniel, J. Scott Duvall, and C. Marvin Pate. *Dictionary of Biblical Prophecy and End Times*. Grand Rapids: Zondervan, 2007.

Hitchcock, Mark. *Bible Prophecy*. Wheaton: Tyndale House, 1999.

———. *The Coming Islamic Invasion of Israel*. Sisters: Multnomah, 2002.

———. *Iran: The Coming Crisis*. Sisters: Multnomah, 2006.

———. *Is America in Bible Prophecy?* Sisters: Multnomah, 2002.

———. *The Late Great United States*. Colorado Springs: Multnomah, 2009.

———. *The Second Coming of Babylon*. Sisters: Multnomah, 2003.

Hodge, Charles. *Systematic Theology*. Grand Rapids: Eerdmans, 1952.

Hoyt, Herman. *The End Times*. Chicago: Moody, 1969.

Ice, Thomas, and Timothy Demy. *Prophecy Watch*. Eugene: Harvest House, 1998.

———. *What the Bible Says About Heaven and Eternity*. Grand Rapids: Kregel, 2000.

———. *When the Trumpet Sounds*. Eugene: Harvest House, 1995.

Ice, Thomas, and Randall Price. *Ready to Rebuild: The Imminent Plan to Rebuild the Last Days Temple*. Eugene: Harvest House, 1992.

Ladd, George Eldon. *I Believe in the Resurrection of Jesus*. Grand Rapids: Eerdmans, 1975.

LaHaye, Tim. *The Beginning of the End*. Wheaton: Tyndale, 1991.

———. *The Coming Peace in the Middle East*. Grand Rapids: Zondervan, 1984.

LaHaye, Tim, ed. *Prophecy Study Bible*. Chattanooga: AMG, 2001.

LaHaye, Tim, and Ed Hindson, eds. *The Popular Bible Prophecy Commentary*. Eugene: Harvest House, 2006.

———. *The Popular Encyclopedia of Bible Prophecy*. Eugene: Harvest House, 2004.

LaHaye, Tim, and Thomas Ice. *Charting the End Times*. Eugene: Harvest House, 2001.

LaHaye, Tim, and Jerry Jenkins. *Are We Living in the End Times?* Wheaton: Tyndale, 1999.

MacArthur, John, ed. *The MacArthur Study Bible*. Nashville: Thomas Nelson, 2003.

MacDonald, W., and A. Farstad. *Believer's Bible Commentary*. Nashville: Thomas Nelson, 1997.

Marsden, George. *Jonathan Edwards: A Life*. New Haven: Yale University, 2003.

McDowell, Josh. *Evidence that Demands a Verdict*. San Bernardino: Campus Crusade for Christ, 1972.

Pentecost, J. Dwight. *Things to Come*. Grand Rapids: Zondervan, 1964.

———. *The Words and Works of Jesus Christ*. Grand Rapids: Zondervan, 1978.

Price, Randall. *Fast Facts on the Middle East conflict*. Eugene: Harvest House, 2003.

———. *Unholy War*. Eugene: Harvest House, 2001.

Rhodes, Ron. *Christ Before the Manger: The Life and Times of the Preincarnate Christ*. Grand Rapids: Baker, 1992.

———. *Christianity According to the Bible*. Eugene: Harvest House, 2006.

———. *The Coming Oil Storm*. Eugene: Harvest House, 2010.

———. *The Middle East Conflict: What You Need to Know*. Eugene: Harvest House, 2009.

———. *Northern Storm Rising: Russia, Iran, and the Emerging End-Times Military Coalition Against Israel*. Eugene: Harvest House, 2008.

———. *The Popular Dictionary of Bible Prophecy*. Eugene: Harvest House, 2010.

———. *The Topical Guide of Bible Prophecy*. Eugene: Harvest House, 2010.

Rosenberg, Joel. *Epicenter: Why Current Rumblings in the Middle East Will Change Your Future*. Carol Stream: Tyndale, 2006.

Ruthven, Jon Mark. *The Prophecy That Is Shaping History: New Research on Ezekiel's Vision of the End*. Fairfax: Xulon, 2003.

Ryrie, Charles. *Basic Theology*. Wheaton: Victor, 1986.

———. *Dispensationalism Today*. Chicago: Moody, 1965.

Ryrie, Charles, ed. *The Ryrie Study Bible*. Chicago: Moody Press, 2011.

Sanders, J. Oswald. *Heaven: Better by Far*. Grand Rapids: Discovery House, 1993.

Shelley, Bruce. *Theology for Ordinary People*. Downers Grove: InterVarsity, 1994.

Showers, Renald. *Maranatha: Our Lord Come!* Bellmawr: The Friends of Israel Gospel Ministry, 1995.

Thomas, F.W. *Masters of Deception*. Grand Rapids: Baker Books, 1983.

Toussaint, Stanley. *Behold the King: A Study of Matthew*. Grand Rapids: Kregel, 2005.

Unger, Merrill F. *Beyond the Crystal Ball*. Chicago: Moody, 1978.

Walvoord, John F. *End Times*. Nashville: Word, 1998.

———. *Jesus Christ Our Lord*. Chicago: Moody, 1980.

———. *The Millennial Kingdom*. Grand Rapids: Zondervan, 1975.

———. *The Prophecy Knowledge Handbook*. Wheaton: Victor, 1990.

———. *The Return of the Lord*. Grand Rapids: Zondervan, 1979.

Walvoord, John F., and Mark Hitchcock. *Armageddon, Oil, and Terror*. Carol Stream: Tyndale House, 2007.

Walvoord, John F., and John E. Walvoord. *Armageddon, Oil, and the Middle East Crisis*. Grand Rapids: Zondervan, 1975.

Yamauchi, Edwin. *Foes from the Northern Frontier: Invading Hordes from the Russian Steppes*. Eugene: Wipf and Stock, 1982.

Notes

Chapter 1: Introduction to Biblical Prophecy

1. Credit goes to my common conference associate Norman Geisler for this memorable phraseology.
2. Thomas Constable, "Notes on 2 Timothy." Available online at www.soniclight.com/constable/notes/pdf/2timothy.pdf.
3. Cited in Arnold Fruchtenbaum, *The Footsteps of the Messiah* (San Antonio: Ariel Ministries, 2003), n.p.
4. Fruchtenbaum, *The Footsteps of the Messiah*.
5. Genesis 12:1-3; 15:18-21; 35:10-12; see also Isaiah 60:18,21; Jeremiah 23:6; 24:5-6; 30:18; 31:31-34; 32:37-40; 33:6-9; Ezekiel 28:25-26; 34:11-12; 36:24-26; 37; 39:28; Hosea 3:4-5; Joel 2:18-29; Amos 9:14-15; Micah 2:12; 4:6-7; Zephaniah 3:19-20; Zechariah 8:7-8; 13:8-9.

Chapter 2: Prior to the Tribulation

1. Thomas Ice, "Consistent Biblical Futurism (Part 4)," *Bible Prophecy Blog*, January 21, 2011. www.bibleprophecyblog.com/2011/01/consistent-biblical-futurism-part-4.html.
2. Joel Rosenberg, *Epicenter* (Carol Stream: Tyndale House, 2006), p. 27.
3. Some of this information about the gradual return of Jews to their homeland is based on James Combs, "Israel in Two Centuries," in *Prophecy Study Bible*, ed. Tim LaHaye (Chattanooga: AMG Publishers, 2001), p. 970.
4. Stephen Leeb, *The Coming Economic Collapse* (New York: Warner, 2006), p. 30.

Chapter 3: The Rapture

1. Renald Showers, *Maranatha: Our Lord Come!* (Bellmawr: Friends of Israel, 1995), p. 214.
2. Arnold Fruchtenbaum, *The Footsteps of the Messiah* (San Antonio: Ariel Ministries, 2003), n.p.
3. Cited in Showers, *Maranatha: Our Lord Come!*, p. 197.
4. Showers, *Maranatha: Our Lord Come!*, p. 128. See also Fruchtenbaum, *The Footsteps of the Messiah*.

234   THE END TIMES IN CHRONOLOGICAL ORDER

Chapter 4: The Results of the Rapture

1. John F. Walvoord, "Revelation," in *The Bible Knowledge Commentary*, *New Testament Edition*, ed. John Walvoord and Roy Zuck (Colorado Springs: David C. Cook, 1983), n.p.

2. Paul Feinberg, "2 Thessalonians 2 and the Rapture," in *When the Trumpet Sounds*, ed. Thomas Ice and Timothy Demy (Eugene: Harvest House, 1995), p. 307.

3. Arnold Fruchtenbaum, *The Footsteps of the Messiah* (San Antonio: Ariel Ministries, 2003), n.p.

4. Fruchtenbaum, *The Footsteps of the Messiah*.

5. Feinberg, "2 Thessalonians 2 and the Rapture," p. 307.

6. Feinberg, "2 Thessalonians 2 and the Rapture," p. 307.

7. Thomas Constable, "2 Thessalonians," in *The Popular Bible Prophecy Commentary*, ed. Tim LaHaye and Ed Hindson (Eugene: Harvest House, 2006), p. 455.

8. Constable, "2 Thessalonians," p. 455.

9. Mal Couch, "Restrainer," in *The Popular Encyclopedia of Bible Prophecy*, ed. Tim LaHaye and Ed Hindson (Eugene: Harvest House, 2004), p. 325.

10. Mark Hitchcock, *Is the Antichrist Alive Today?* (Colorado Springs: Multnomah, 2002), p. 83.

11. Couch, "Restrainer," p. 325.

12. Cited in David Jeremiah, *The Coming Economic Armageddon* (New York: Faith Words, 2010), p. 114.

13. Feinberg, "2 Thessalonians 2 and the Rapture," p. 308.

14. William MacDonald and Arthur L. Farstad, *Believer's Bible Commentary* (Nashville: Thomas Nelson, 1995), n.p.

15. J. Oswald Sanders, *Heaven: Better by Far* (Grand Rapids: Discovery House, 1993), p. 91.

16. Jon Courson, *Jon Courson's Application Commentary* (Nashville: Thomas Nelson, 2003), p. 1118.

17. Albert Barnes, *Notes on the New Testament*, vol. 8, *2 Corinthians* (Grand Rapids: Baker, 1996), p. 105.

18. Courson, *Jon Courson's Application Commentary*, p. 1118.

19. Paul Powell, *When the Hurt Won't Go Away* (Wheaton: Victor, 1986), p. 119.

Chapter 5: The Church with Christ in Heaven

1. Arnold Fruchtenbaum, *The Footsteps of the Messiah* (San Antonio: Ariel Ministries, 2003), n.p.

2. Thomas Constable, "Notes on Revelation." Available online at www.soniclight.com/constable/notes/pdf/revelation.pdf.

3. John MacArthur, *The MacArthur Study Bible* (Nashville: Thomas Nelson, 2006), n.p.

Chapter 6: The Invasion of Israel

1. Joel Rosenberg, *Epicenter* (Carol Stream: Tyndale House, 2006), pp. 68-69.

2. Arnold Fruchtenbaum, *The Footsteps of the Messiah* (San Antonio: Ariel Ministries, 2003), n.p.

3. Thomas Ice, "Ezekiel 38 and 39," part 1. Available online at www.bibleprophecyblog.com/2011/01/ezekiel-38-39-part-1.html.

4. Ice, "Ezekiel 38 and 39," part 1.

5. John F. Walvoord, "Revelation," in *The Bible Knowledge Commentary, New Testament Edition,* ed. John Walvoord and Roy Zuck (Colorado Springs: David C. Cook, 1983), n.p.

6. Joel Rosenberg, *Epicenter* (Carol Stream: Tyndale House, 2006), pp. 163-64.

7. Arnold Fruchtenbaum, *The Footsteps of the Messiah.*

Chapter 7: The Beginning of the Tribulation: The Emergence of the Antichrist

1. Renald Showers, *Maranatha: Our Lord Come!* (Bellmawr: Friends of Israel, 1995), p. 21.

2. See John 14:1-3; Romans 8:19; 1 Corinthians 1:7-8; 15:51-53; 16:22; Philippians 3:20-21; Colossians 3:4; 1 Thessalonians 1:10; 4:13-18; 2 Thessalonians 2:1,3; Titus 2:13; Hebrews 9:28; 1 Peter 1:7,13; 5:4; 1 John 2:28–3:2; Revelation 2:25; 3:10.

3. Some prophecy scholars associate the ten kings with the world government. See Arnold Fruchtenbaum, *The Footsteps of the Messiah* (San Antonio: Ariel Ministries, 2003), n.p.

Chapter 8: The Beginning of the Tribulation: The Temple and Signs of the End

1. John F. Walvoord, "Revelation," in *The Bible Knowledge Commentary, New Testament Edition,* ed. John Walvoord and Roy Zuck (Colorado Springs: David C. Cook, 1983), n.p.

Chapter 9: The First Half of the Tribulation: The Lamb and His Witnesses

1. John F. Walvoord, "Revelation," in *The Bible Knowledge Commentary, New Testament Edition,* ed. John Walvoord and Roy Zuck (Colorado Springs: David C. Cook, 1983), n.p.

2. See Arnold Fruchtenbaum, *The Footsteps of the Messiah* (San Antonio: Ariel Ministries, 2003), n.p.

Chapter 10: The First Half of the Tribulation: Judgments, Martyrdom, and Apostasy

1. J.I. Packer, *Knowing God* (Downers Grove: InterVarsity Press, 1983), p. 126.

2. Thomas Constable, "Notes on Revelation." Available online at www.soniclight.com/constable/notes/pdf/revelation.pdf.

Chapter 11: The Midpoint of the Tribulation

1. John F. Walvoord, "Revelation," in *The Bible Knowledge Commentary, New Testament Edition,* ed. John Walvoord and Roy Zuck (Colorado Springs: David C. Cook, 1983), n.p.

2. William MacDonald and Arthur L. Farstad, *Believer's Bible Commentary* (Nashville: Thomas Nelson, 1995), n.p.

3. Arnold Fruchtenbaum, *The Footsteps of the Messiah* (San Antonio: Ariel Ministries, 2003), n.p.

4. Fruchtenbaum, *The Footsteps of the Messiah.*

5. Fruchtenbaum, *The Footsteps of the Messiah.*

6. Walvoord, "Revelation."

7. Arnold Fruchtenbaum, *The Footsteps of the Messiah.*

8. Thomas Constable, "Notes on Revelation." Available online at www.soniclight.com/constable/notes/pdf/revelation.pdf.

9. Thomas Constable, "Notes on Revelation."

10. William MacDonald and Arthur L. Farstad, *The Believer's Bible Commentary.*

11. Walvoord, "Revelation."

12. Walvoord, "Revelation."

13. William MacDonald and Arthur L. Farstad, *The Believer's Bible Commentary*.

14. Arnold Fruchtenbaum, *The Footsteps of the Messiah*.

Chapter 12: The Second Half of the Tribulation

1. Renald Showers, *Maranatha: Our Lord Come!* (Bellmawr: Friends of Israel, 1995), p. 43.

2. Irenaeus, *Adversus Haereses*, book 5, chapter 30.4.

3. Cited in Renald Showers, *Maranatha: Our Lord Come!*, p. 50.

4. Showers, *Maranatha*, p. 50.

5. Thomas Ice and Timothy Demy, *The Coming Cashless Society* (Eugene: Harvest House, 1996), pp. 125-26, 80.

6. Arnold Fruchtenbaum, *The Footsteps of the Messiah* (San Antonio: Ariel Ministries, 2003), n.p.

7. Mark Hitchcock, *Cashless: Bible Prophecy, Economic Chaos, and the Future Financial Order* (Eugene: Harvest House, 2010), pp. 163-64.

8. Cited in Thomas Ice and Timothy Demy, *Fast Facts on Bible Prophecy from A to Z* (Eugene: Harvest House, 2004), p. 129.

9. John MacArthur, *The MacArthur Study Bible* (Nashville: Thomas Nelson, 2006). See the note on Revelation 13:16.

10. John F. Walvoord, *The Prophecy Knowledge Handbook* (Wheaton: Victor Books, 1990), n.p.

11. Cited in Ice and Demy, *The Coming Cashless Society*, p. 132.

12. William MacDonald and Arthur L. Farstad, *Believer's Bible Commentary* (Nashville: Thomas Nelson, 1995), n.p.

Chapter 13: The End of the Tribulation

1. John F. Walvoord, "Revelation," in *The Bible Knowledge Commentary, New Testament Edition*, ed. John Walvoord and Roy Zuck (Colorado Springs: David C. Cook, 1983), n.p.

2. Arnold Fruchtenbaum, *The Footsteps of the Messiah* (San Antonio: Ariel Ministries, 2003), n.p.

Chapter 14: After the Tribulation, Before the Millennial Kingdom

1. Renald Showers, *Maranatha: Our Lord Come!* (Bellmawr: Friends of Israel, 1995), pp. 57-58.

2. Stanley Toussaint, *Behold the King: A Study of Matthew* (Grand Rapids: Kregel, 2005), p. 291.

3. Merrill F. Unger, *Beyond the Crystal Ball* (Chicago: Moody, 1978), pp. 134-35.

4. J. Dwight Pentecost, *The Words and Works of Jesus Christ* (Grand Rapids: Zondervan, 1978), p. 410. See also J. Dwight Pentecost, *Things to Come* (Grand Rapids: Zondervan, 1978), p. 418.

5. "Matthew," in *The Bible Knowledge Commentary, New Testament Edition*, ed. John Walvoord and Roy Zuck (Colorado Springs: David C. Cook, 1983), n.p.

Chapter 15: During the Millennial Kingdom

1. John F. Walvoord, *Major Bible Prophecies* (Grand Rapids: Zondervan, 1991), p. 390.

2. John F. Walvoord, *The Millennial Kingdom* (Grand Rapids: Zondervan, 1981), p. 310.

3. Jerry Hullinger, "The Problem of Animal Sacrifices in Ezekiel 40–48," *Bibliotheca Sacra* 152, July–September 1995, p. 280.

4. Hullinger, "The Problem of Animal Sacrifices in Ezekiel 40–48," p. 289.

5. Walvoord, *The Millennial Kingdom*, p. 307.

Chapter 17: The Eternal State

1. Charles F. Pfeiffer and Everett F. Harrison, eds., *The Wycliffe Bible Commentary* (Chicago: Moody, 1974), p. 1257.

2. F.W. Thomas, *Masters of Deception* (Grand Rapids: Baker Books, 1983), p. 21.

3. Albert Barnes, "Revelation," in *Notes on the New Testament* (Grand Rapids: Baker, 1996), p. 454.

4. John MacArthur, *The Glory of Heaven* (Wheaton: Crossway, 1996), p. 90.

5. Cited in J. Oswald Sanders, *Heaven: Better by Far* (Grand Rapids: Discovery House, 1993), p. 131.

6. Sanders, *Heaven*, p. 134.

7. Cited in Randy Alcorn, *Heaven* (Wheaton: Tyndale, 2004), p. 125.

8. John F. Walvoord, "Revelation," in *The Bible Knowledge Commentary, New Testament Edition*, ed. John Walvoord and Roy Zuck (Colorado Springs: David C. Cook, 1983), n.p.

9. Millard Erickson, *Christian Theology* (Grand Rapids: Baker, 1987), p. 1229.

10. George Marsden, *Jonathan Edwards: A Life* (New Haven: Yale University, 2003), p. 98.

11. Cited in John Walvoord, *The Revelation of Jesus Christ* (Chicago: Moody, 1971), p. 332.

12. Albert Barnes, "Revelation," p. 453.

13. Cited in Tim LaHaye, *Revelation: Illustrated and Made Plain* (Grand Rapids: Zondervan, 1975), p. 315.

14. Bruce Shelley, *Theology for Ordinary People* (Downers Grove: InterVarsity, 1994), p. 212.

15. Cited in "Revelation," *Wycliffe Bible Commentary* (Chicago: Moody, 1960), p. 1524.